"Sam Himelstein walks his talk. Within the pages of this book you will find an important clinical guide to a transformational approach to working with high-risk adolescents. Highly recommend."

—**Elisha Goldstein**, PhD, author of *The Now Effect* and co-author of *A Mindfulness-Based Stress Reduction Workbook*

"Highly illuminating and informative, A Mindfulness-Based Approach to Working with High-Risk Adolescents *is filled with lively clinical vignettes that give you an exciting, in-the-trenches view of how to work skillfully with this challenging population. I would recommend this book to anyone who wants to work with high-risk adolescents. Himelstein knows this work from the inside out!"*

—**Will Kabat-Zinn**, MFTI, Dharma teacher

"Sam Himelstein has done an amazing job of producing the next generation of texts on bringing mindfulness into clinical work. Through a masterful blending of mindfulness, humanistic psychology, and hard-won wisdom drawn from his extensive work with high-risk teens, he has produced a book that is both practical and philosophical. Simply wonderful!"

—**Steven D. Hickman**, PsyD, director, University of California-San Diego Center for Mindfulness

"Sam Himelstein incorporates the rigor of science, the beauty of art, the wisdom of reflection, and years of clinical experience in this pioneering book. A Mindfulness-Based Approach to Working with High-Risk Adolescents *has the power to transform lives."*

—**Shauna L. Shapiro**, PhD, associate professor, Santa Clara University and co-author of *The Art and Science of Mindfulness*

A Mindfulness-Based Approach
to Working with High-Risk Adolescents

A Mindfulness-Based Approach to Working with High-Risk Adolescents is an accessible introduction to a new model of therapy that combines the Buddhist concept of mindfulness with modern trends in psychotherapy. Drawing on years of experience working with at-risk adolescents, the chapters explore ways to develop authentic connections with patients: building relationships, working with resistance, and ways to approach change using mindfulness-based techniques. Real-life interactions and illustrations are used to show how a mindfulness-oriented therapist can approach working with adolescents in individual and group settings, and the book also provides practical suggestions designed for immediate implementation. *A Mindfulness-Based Approach to Working with High-Risk Adolescents* is a must for any mental health professional interested in using mindfulness and other contemplative practices with at-risk youth.

Sam Himelstein, PhD, is associate core faculty at Sofia University, where he teaches graduate courses in research methodology and incorporating mindfulness into psychotherapy. He is also director of clinical services and research at the Mind Body Awareness Project, where he initiates research projects regarding mindfulness and adolescents with other academic professionals. He is a licensed psychologist who works with high-risk adolescents in individual, group, and family therapy. In addition, Himelstein is the executive director of Engaging the Moment, a continuing-education business that trains clinicians in how to approach adolescents with mindfulness and other contemplative practices.

A Mindfulness-Based Approach to Working with High-Risk Adolescents

Sam Himelstein

Routledge
Taylor & Francis Group
NEW YORK AND LONDON

First published 2013
by Routledge
711 Third Avenue, New York, NY 10017

Simultaneously published in the UK
by Routledge
27 Church Road, Hove, East Sussex BN3 2FA

Routledge is an imprint of the Taylor & Francis Group, an informa business

The right of Sam Himelstein to be identified as author of this
work has been asserted by him in accordance with sections
77 and 78 of the Copyright, Designs and Patents Act 1988.

Library of Congress Cataloging in Publication Data
Himelstein, Sam.
  A mindfulness-based approach to working with high-risk
  adolescents/Sam Himelstein.—1 Edition.
  pages cm
  Includes bibliographical references and index.
  1. Problem youth—Psychology. 2. Mindfulness-based
  cognitive therapy. I. Title.
  BF724.H546 2013
  616.89'—dc23
  2012040784
ISBN: 978-0-415-64244-6 (hbk)
ISBN: 978-0-415-64245-3 (pbk)
ISBN: 978-0-203-08085-6 (ebk)

Typeset in Adobe Garamond and Officina Sans by
Florence Production Ltd, Stoodleigh, Devon, UK

Printed and bound in the United States of America by
Walsworth Publishing Company, Marceline, MO.

I dedicate this book to the
many people who have supported me in my
personal and spiritual growth, from my parents and
ancestors, to my clients and colleagues, to my wife Alicia
and son Solomon. This book would not be possible
without you all. Your teachings and grace
shine through me in this work.

Contents

Acknowledgements

I give a special thank you and acknowledgement to the *Journal of Transpersonal Psychology and the Humanistic Psychologist* for giving me permission to use portions of the two articles below in this manuscript:

Himelstein, S. (2011). Engaging the moment with incarcerated youth: An existential–humanistic approach. *The Humanistic Psychologist, 39*, 206–221.

Himelstein, S. (2011). Transpersonal psychotherapy with incarcerated adolescents. *Journal of Transpersonal Psychology, 43*, 1–15.

Introduction

My purpose in writing this book is simple. I wish to provide academic and mental health professionals with a methodology for connecting with high-risk adolescents on an authentic, human-being level. Through this presentation, I hope to assist mental health professionals to learn or deepen their ability to foster the development of self-awareness, conscious living, and choicefulness among their adolescent clients. I hope that the therapeutic experiences and methods that I review in the following pages will be explored, attempted, and even critiqued and improved in such a way that mental health professionals working in different settings with multiple theoretical orientations can competently engage the challenging but rewarding work with this population of young people.

Clinical work with high-risk adolescents is not only challenging at times, but also in need of diverse approaches. For example, literature on psychotherapy with incarcerated adolescents is limited to primarily manualized cognitive-based group interventions (Guerra, Kim, & Boxer, 2008), motivational interviewing (Ginsburg, Mann, Rotgers, & Weekes, 2002), solution-focused therapy (Corcoran, 1997), and multiple system approaches (Schaeffer & Borduin, 2005). Although most of these approaches maintain some empirical support, they often leave clinicians without specific instruction on how to engage this population clinically. Thus, my intention is to discuss in detail the intricacies of the therapeutic process with high-risk adolescents: from developing an authentic relationship to confronting risky and life-threatening behavior. This is done, I believe, with the assumption that an authentic therapist–client relationship is the base for the ability to explore in depth the conscious, semiconscious, and subconscious processes that contribute to what is commonsensically known as personality. It is through this exploration and enhancement of self-awareness that true choice and growth can occur. Thus, I term this deep exploration between the client and therapist as "engaging the moment." The verb "to engage" is active, suggesting that this is a moment-by-moment exploration that develops and changes alongside present-moment experience. It is this awareness of the moment-by-moment self that becomes engaged, from a base of an authentic relationship, and through which growth and change can occur. This happens with guidance, not forcefulness on the therapist's part, and is truly engaged at the choice of the client.

Before journeying through the following chapters, there are some basic but important assumptions I hold that should be taken into account as a reader. First, as a clinician, I strive to be culturally sensitive and aware of the power dynamics that inherently arise while working with high-risk adolescents. I believe the single most important aspect of working with this population is viewing them as human beings. If you get caught up in treating them like children, stripping them of autonomy and independence —which they are striving so hard for in this life stage—your attempts at facilitating true growth will ultimately fail. Adolescents are searching for connections with adults who trust their experience and wisdom as truth; they are not looking for someone to tell them that what they have been doing is wrong! If this concept is difficult for you, I urge you to read through the following pages with openness and a sense of exploration while consistently thinking back to your own experiences as an adolescent and your interactions at that age with adults.

Second, it is also important that I clearly define the population that I work with and am envisioning while writing this book. *High-risk adolescent* can be descriptive of a number of adolescent populations. Here, I use the term mostly to represent adolescents who live in impoverished neighborhoods and deal with all of the accompanying social issues (e.g., violence, crime, substance abuse, poverty, gangs, etc.). However, I have worked with adolescents who live in wealthy neighborhoods and who nevertheless deal with a number of similar, along with some different, issues (e.g., substance abuse, suicide, achievement issues, belongingness, etc.) and extend the term to this population, as well. Basically, high-risk adolescents are those who get into significant trouble, range approximately in age from 13–19, have significant delinquency issues, engage in criminal behavior, suffer from substance abuse and dependence, may be incarcerated, and may experience trauma and involvement with gangs. While there have been some strong literary pieces (e.g., Taffel, 2005) on working with *troubled teens* (i.e., adolescents who have some delinquency and behavioral issues but tend not to be too involved in the judicial system) that have influenced my work, I speak here to a population that is consistently at odds with the law and authority figures. Clients that I do not address in this book are adolescents who suffer from severe mental illness such as schizophrenia and other psychotic symptoms, or severe mood or personality disorders that may best be approached with a combination of psychotherapy and pharmaco-therapy.

Third, although I define the population that I am writing about as high-risk adolescents, please attempt not to ascribe each of the clients a general personality type. Oftentimes, when I train clinicians in the community who are just beginning clinical work or are switching to clinical work with this population, they ascribe to the population the hard attitude, thug-mannered, gangbanger persona of one who does not care about anything in the world. Alternatively, I have also worked with clinicians who have had a "You have it so well, why are you doing all this?" approach to adolescents from high-income neighborhoods and thus invalidate their issues as based on external socio-economic status. It is my hope that, no matter the client, or the sub-population clientele, clinicians approach their clients with *beginner's mind*, or the ability to approach them with open-ness, curiosity, and nonjudgment. I have met clients who fit the stereo-typical personality associated with a gangster (e.g., hardened attitude, prideful, tough, etc.), and I have also met gangsters with soft, warm, and approachable personalities, as well as every possible presentation in between. Thus, it is of utmost importance that, when working with this population, you as a clinician are open to the diversity of clients who will enter into therapy with you. This is not to say that you will not see certain behavioral themes arise (e.g., substance abuse, delinquency, gang activity), but rather that the contextual factors that have led to such behavior have, in my experience, been just as diverse as in any other population I have worked with.

Fourth, I want to suggest that, although the principles and practices I write about in this book are geared toward clinicians working with high-risk adolescents, I believe they are equally applicable to any client population, as well as to any human relationship, for that matter. I write through the lens of working with high-risk adolescents because they are the population that I am passionate about serving. In my work with them I feel whole and complete; my understanding of my own spirituality and personal growth reveals itself to me in its purest nature. This is why I feel passionate about writing from such a perspective. The qualities that I highlight in the following chapters—human connection, authenticity, acceptance, love, healthy boundaries, and courage—are fundamental aspects of the human condition and necessary for human growth.

Finally, I believe it important to define mindfulness as I experience it. We are in an age in which literature on mindfulness in the Western world is exponentially increasing and, therefore, we are in need of the paradigmatic positioning of different mindfulness traditions and practices. It is my hope that, in the near future, mindfulness authors will in their practice name their paradigms, including any biases, philosophical underpinnings, and so forth, just as qualitative researchers do currently with their research. This will shed light on the context that influences each author, which is why I present mine here.

While I do ascribe to the now infamous "Paying attention in a particular way: on purpose, in the present-moment, and nonjudgmentally" (Kabat-Zinn, 1994) as a definition of mindfulness, I also believe that mindfulness is heavily intertwined with the practice of authenticity. My training in the existential–humanistic stream of psychotherapy in the tradition of Jim Bugental and Myrtle Heery has no doubt influenced my paradigm. However, given that I have always viewed my therapy training as a spiritual practice, I see no conflict in the merging of the existential–humanistic and Buddhist traditions. In fact, when examined at the core, they have much similarity. Therefore, I view the practice of mindfulness as the practice of present-moment awareness tuned to authentic experience, in a range extending from the core conditions that create and maintain suffering to the transient nature of personal ego structure. In its manifestation on the level of primary experience (e.g., the realm of this world that encompasses the things we must do in order to walk through life), I view the practice of mindfulness as the ability to be present and de-identified with thoughts, emotions, and sensations.

In its deepest manifestation, I view mindfulness as a consistent return to the pure awareness that underlies the primary awareness from which most human beings function daily. This is a level of awareness that, in my experience, precludes the ability to think, "I am present right now." It is a layer deeper in which awareness, being, and nowness are collapsed into an organic entity in which wisdom and knowledge are manifested through media other than rational thought. Because of both types of the experiences described, the phrase that I most resonate with is *authentic self-awareness*. Through this literary piece on therapy with high-risk adolescents, I offer to the academic and mental health profession a methodology for engaging both our own and our clients' authentic self-awareness and core personality function.

SYNOPSIS OF THE CHAPTERS TO FOLLOW

I have organized this book into three major parts: the *context* related to working with high-risk adolescents, which includes the philosophical tenets that underlie a mindfulness model of therapy and the intricacies in developing and maintaining an authentic client–therapist relationship; the *content* that clinicians can expect to arise, including the exploration of meaning, worldview, and core themes; and foundational *skills* that can be used, including group facilitation, eliciting present-moment awareness from the process of therapy, and teaching mindfulness to high-risk adolescents.

In order for readers to adequately understand the stance I take in therapy with high-risk adolescents, I believe it necessary to present my philosophical paradigm of operation. In a manner similar to how qualitative researchers position themselves in regard to ontology, epistemology, axiology, and methodology, I, too, will progress through this book positioning myself with a greater paradigm of the human condition. I will start with theory and progressively move toward more pragmatic, detailed methodologies for engaging high-risk adolescents in clinical settings, including the teaching of specific mindfulness practices and activities. I use real transcripts and examples from my practice, assigning pseudonyms and altering identifying information to conceal their identities.

Part One: Context

As was stated above, I begin this discussion with a presentation of my ontology: a mindfulness model of therapy as it relates to work with high-risk adolescents (Chapter 1). The incorporation of mindfulness into therapy has progressed over the past four decades as a result of an onslaught of mostly postpositivist research and thinking, and, as a consequence, researchers and therapists objectify its use in therapy, most reducing it in their understanding to the status of one of their "techniques," rather than adopting it as a more holistic approach to working with other human beings. I will briefly review the current uses of mindfulness in Western therapy and expand upon this paradigm to incorporate a more holistic approach. Existentialist, Buddhist, and humanistic theories will be drawn upon to clearly define and support this holistic paradigm of mindfulness therapy and will provide specific examples and citing of research to suggest why it is important in working with high-risk adolescents.

After the presentation of a holistic mindfulness therapy paradigm, I then turn to the intricacies of developing an authentic therapist–client relationship, providing specific examples of case illustrations and transcripts (Chapter 2).

The development of an authentic therapist–client relationship with high-risk adolescents is particularly important in order to confront and challenge one's clients (Chapter 3). The chapter on this process is concerned with the relationship between authenticity and *resistance patterns*. Bugental (1965, 1987, 1999) uses the term *resistances* or *resistance structures* to refer to the defensive mechanisms that are encapsulated within what he calls the self-and-world construct system: the way in which we as human beings relate to the world. I build on the engagement of such resistance structures and suggest them as "protective" mechanisms developed by high-risk adolescents that, rather than being seen as needing to be eradicated, are held by the therapist to be honored mechanisms that protect the client from trauma.

Following Chapter 3, an approach to the difficult feat of using human connection and concern to guide your client toward growth and/or change is presented (Chapter 4). I say *difficult* because therapists often can get into "preach" mode, a presentation that high-risk youth are not only accustomed to, but are practiced, when encountering it, to shut down. Human connection and concern highlights the paradox that pushing your client to change will only hurt your rapport (unless your client wants to change, of course) and that much skillfulness is needed in order to successfully use your concern to guide him or her along the path of change.

Part Two: Content

This brief section begins with a discussion on attention to spirituality, meaning-making, and building an authentic worldview, and how such processes are key in the development of a positive relationship to the world (Chapter 5). This section ends with a discussion of the core themes that can be expected to arise when working with this population and how they are related to the philosophical foundations of a mindfulness model of therapy (Chapter 6). Case illustrations in these chapters are more developed to exemplify these content areas.

Part Three: Skills

Chapters 7, 8, and 9 all focus on practical activities, interventions, or methods I have found useful in working with high-risk adolescents. The section begins with methodologies for sound group facilitation, whether it be manualized or process-oriented, with high-risk adolescents (Chapter 7). A number of practical principles will be presented that can be adapted to any group. Next, the focus will move to specific clinical skills that can be used to elicit the client's authentic subjective awareness in session (Chapter 8). I will present a conceptual framework using the foundations of mindfulness as a tracking system that can guide the awareness of the therapist. Finally, the explicit teaching of mindfulness will be presented in the last chapter (Chapter 9). I have deliberately positioned this chapter at the end of the book to highlight the need to prioritize the relational factors in which a mindfulness model may influence therapy over the isolated teaching of mindfulness as a "technique." In this chapter, I discuss the introduction of mindfulness, the clarification of the goal of mindfulness practice with this population, and ten principles I have found useful in explicitly teaching mindfulness to high-risk adolescents. I save specific exercises and mindfulness-based activities for the appendix located after the concluding chapter of this book (Appendix A).

In sum, what I am proposing is an ontology for a model of mindfulness in therapy in which the authentic relationship is used as the platform from which growth might occur. My intention is to influence the professionals who work with this population, and my hope is that other experts in the field will begin to address this often swept-under-the-rug clinical population by writing about detailed clinical experiences.

P A R T

CONTEXT

A Mindfulness Model of Therapy

Research on the efficacy of mindfulness-based interventions has progressed over the last four decades, and, with the development of the "evidence-based" movement in psychology, many clinicians have sought training in mindfulness and incorporated it into their practice. There have been few books (Germer, Siegel, & Fulton, 2005; Hick & Bien, 2008; Shapiro & Carlson, 2009) that explicitly discuss different areas of application for which the practice of mindfulness can be applied in clinical interactions. Shapiro and Carlson (2009) and Germer et al. (2005) both suggest that mindfulness manifests in therapy as *mindfulness-informed therapy*, in which the philosophical principles of mindfulness can be applied to therapy; *mindfulness-based therapy*, in which therapists explicitly teach their clients formal and informal mindfulness techniques they can employ to cope with daily stressors; and *therapist mindfulness*, in which the therapist him or herself practices mindfulness in order to build therapeutic presence, develop self-awareness, and practice self-care. Of these three areas, mindfulness-based interventions have overwhelmingly received the most attention (Baer, 2006) in the field, followed by an increased awareness of therapist mindfulness (Hick & Bien, 2008; Siegel, 2010). Because of our current paradigm's focus on proving interventions to be efficacious, one consequence has been a culture of using mindfulness in therapy simply as a "technique" (i.e., a solution to a problem) and rarely anything more. And although mindfulness as a technique is positive (e.g., this technique has proven helpful for many populations) and an integral part of the intersection between mindfulness and therapy, it is only one aspect of the mindfulness model of therapy that I present within these pages.

The goal of this chapter is to present a comprehensive mindfulness model of therapy as it relates to clinical work with high-risk adolescents. I draw heavily on Buddhist and existential concepts, my direct and literary teachers, and personal experience. My goal is not to present *the* model of mindfulness but rather one model, which will hopefully be critiqued and expanded upon by other mindful therapists. In a review based upon my agreement with previous authors (e.g., Germer et al., 2005; Shapiro & Carlson, 2009), I review the importance of a mindfulness model as it applies to the philosophical assumptions of therapy, to the direct teaching of mindfulness both formally through mediation and informally, and to the application of mindfulness for therapists themselves to develop personally and professionally. Further, I add the area of *process mindfulness*, or the awareness of the therapist as focused on both the relational dynamics between the client and therapist and the objective markers that point toward the subjective state of the client. Additionally, because of their overwhelming absence in the literature (for two exceptions, see Germer et al., 2005 and Shapiro & Carlson, 2009), in this chapter I focus heavily on the philosophical foundations and the aspects of therapist mindfulness in this model that apply to working with high-risk adolescents. I expand on the direct teaching of mindfulness (i.e., mindfulness-based interventions), therapist mindfulness, and process mindfulness throughout this book.

FOUR APPLICATIONS OF MINDFULNESS IN THERAPY

Mindfulness-Based Interventions

I use the term mindfulness-based intervention here—in alignment with previous authors (e.g., Germer et al., 2005; Shapiro & Carlson, 2009)—to suggest the explicit teaching of mindfulness, formally through mediative practices or informally through psychoeducation, to adolescent clients. For example, a therapist employing a mindfulness-based intervention might teach a client dealing with stress a 5-minute meditation, and then practice it with that client. The therapist may further practice that meditation along with the client in therapy and progress to more advanced and longer periods of meditation. Alongside the formal teaching and practice of mindfulness, the therapist might also discuss other situations in which mindfulness can be applied in daily life outside of meditation practice (e.g., informal teaching of mindfulness) and practice that with the client in session.

As I mentioned above, mindfulness-based interventions have over-whelmingly received the most attention in applying mindfulness to therapy (Baer, 2006; Germer et al., 2005; Shapiro & Carlson, 2009). There are a growing number of studies that have investigated the impact of mindfulness-based interventions with diverse adolescent populations, including psychiatric outpatients (Biegel, Brown, Shapiro, & Schubert, 2009), public middle school students (Wall, 2005), HIV-infected adolescents (Sibinga et al., 2007), and incarcerated adolescents (Himelstein, Hastings, Shapiro, & Heery, 2012a, 2012b), and they all suggest that mindfulness is both useful and feasible.

On the one hand, explicitly teaching mindfulness to your client can be a limited form of application: for example, let's say your client is stressed out and you want to help him solve his problem (e.g., reduce his stress) by teaching him mindfulness. This type of incorporation is by no means negative (especially if it's helping your client), but often emerges from the mindfulness-based therapy trainings that attempt to certify clinicians (in a short amount of time) to teach mindfulness and contributes to a limited view of how mindfulness can be applied in therapy. On the other hand, explicitly teaching your client mindfulness can be used at an extremely deep level in therapy. For example, consider the situation in which you have an adolescent client who is trying to make meaning in her life and is committed to personal and spiritual growth and self-care. Now, you are looked to as a mentor who will guide your client along a path of mindful and self-awareness development. This is where there is the potential for deep transmissions of wisdom, and it requires a highly trained clinician and meditator.

Process Mindfulness

Another application of mindfulness to therapy is being mindful of the process level of therapy in the moment, during the session. This area of mindfulness rarely receives attention in regard to incorporating mindfulness into therapy (for two exceptions, see Hick & Bien, 2008; Safran & Muran, 2000). Process mindfulness incorporates the awareness of the therapist (something I'll cover in the next section) in that it encapsulates the moment experiencing—countertransference, awareness of *metacommunications* (implicit communications), and so on—during sessions, and expands to the intersubjective relating that is operational between therapist and client. A therapist utilizing this application of mindfulness may be contemplating how the content of what is being said in therapy is impacting the present-moment relationship and may be focusing on the client's present-moment experiencing rather than the background story. The present moment is highlighted by the therapist and used as a tool to unearth the authentic subjective experience of the client.

Alongside the above practices, process mindfulness is also an avenue through which to apply the four foundations of mindfulness to therapy. The four foundations of mindfulness practice (Anayalo, 2010)—the body, feeling tone (positive, negative, neutral), mind states (encapsulating emotions), and dharmas (mechanisms of personality)—serve as a methodology to engage a particular aspect of experience in the present moment. For example, if you have a client who taps his leg, bites his nails, slouches, or engages in any number of patterned behaviors while explaining his experience, you have the potential to explore that behavior as it relates to his subjective state. This also applies to whether or not there may be a patterned occurrence of feeling tones (i.e., often positive or negative judgments of experience) and emotions (which are both encapsulated in mechanisms of personality, among other things).

Therapist Mindfulness

Probably the second most referenced application of mindfulness to therapy is the clinician's own personal mindfulness practice. I contend that this application is most important to the development of clinical skills in therapists, given its gift to the therapist of the ability to transcend mindful paradigms of therapy and the pragmatic skills it encompasses, regardless of the therapist's theoretical orientation. Briefly, this application of mindfulness emphasizes that the therapist commits to personal growth and self-awareness; the development of presence; and mindfulness of countertransference, personal anxiety, and other uncomfortable feelings that result from client interactions, along with the development of self-care practices. Therapist mindfulness emphasizes the sharpening of the therapist herself or himself as the primary "tool" through which therapy is practiced. Being more present to clients, and to personal self-care, is extremely important in this field, given that working with high-risk adolescents can be extremely challenging and, at times, without reward. (For in-depth reviews on therapist mindfulness, consult the texts by Germer (2009), Shapiro and Carlson (2009) and Siegel (2010).)

One element that all of the aforementioned texts, as well as this book, have in common is the importance of personal practice. That is, if a therapist chooses to teach mindfulness meditation directly to her or his client (e.g., to use mindfulness-based interventions) it is imperative that he or she have a personal meditation practice and be continually working toward a progression down the mindful path. A therapist who teaches outside of the scope of personal experience does his or her clients a disservice in not being able to answer questions from experience and will indubitably face challenges in guiding the client forward. Furthermore, the therapist's personal practice of mindfulness is one of the most important factors in successfully working with high-risk adolescents. In viewing therapist mindfulness as the harnessing of skills and qualities that sharpen therapists themselves, there are some particular qualities that develop during sustained mindfulness and self-awareness practices that are imperative to working with high-risk adolescents. Such qualities include authenticity, an intention toward human connection, and an authentic view on locus of control and behavioral change.

Authenticity

One of the most important factors in developing quality relationships with high-risk adolescents is the degree to which the clinician is authentic—that is, that the clinician feels comfortable in his or her own skin, has sufficient ego strength, and is not overtly concerned with being liked or impressing her or his clients. For example, an authentic clinician would not adapt a particular style of speech or sub-cultural behavior simply for the purpose of building a relationship (e.g., using slang that is specific to the high-risk adolescent subculture he or she is working with). Not only would this be inauthentic, but high-risk adolescents, who already have a keen sense of inauthenticity, could observe such behavior as disrespect, and a therapeutic impasse would probably occur. High-risk adolescents (and any person, for that matter) are much more likely to respect a clinician who is comfortable with him or herself and does not use language outside his or her normal subcultural semantic specifically to create a relationship. For example, I have worked for many years with my friend and colleague Stephen, whom most of our incarcerated adolescent clients would classify as "nerdy." Everything from his body language to his speech could have been, and sometimes was, described as nerdy. He was never incarcerated and did not grow up in a subculture similar to that of the majority of our clients. He could not relate to them through that experience, as I could. However, he is extremely comfortable with who he is; he is an authentic human being, and, because of this, our incarcerated adolescent clients, some of whom are hardened gangsters from impoverished neighborhoods, absolutely love him. He has built some of the most authentic therapist–client relationships I have ever witnessed. They love and respect that he doesn't try to pose as someone he's not. Without such authenticity, the beautiful relationships he's created might not have occurred.

Of final note, there is a deeper implication of the authentic clinician. Not only is authenticity imperative in developing the therapeutic relationship, it also models to the client the practice of authenticity. That is, when high-risk adolescents encounter and spend sufficient time with authentic clinicians, they pick up through osmosis, and sometimes via direct observation, the practice of authenticity, which is a large component of mindfulness practice. Because of this, it is important to view authenticity similarly to mindfulness practice in that it is not an inherent trait that is stagnant; it is a continuous state of awareness that human beings have the potential to access at any given time during the course of therapy and/or life.

Intention for Human Connection

Alongside authenticity, another ingredient in the development of an authentic therapy relationship is the explicit intention to connect, on a human-being level, with the client. Oftentimes therapists get trapped in the idea that what every client needs is a solution to a problem. In the world of working with high-risk adolescents, this often takes the form of either implicitly believing or explicitly telling an adolescent that there is some problem in her or his behavior that needs to be changed. The issue with such a stance is that it automatically aligns you, the therapist, against an authentic connection with the client because he or she will most likely feel judged or controlled. Because of this, it is important to enter therapy with the explicit intention, the explicit treatment objective, to connect with the client on a human-being level rather than trying to change some aspect of the client's behavior. This is done through curiosity, compassion, and skillful self-disclosure (which I discuss in depth in Chapter 2).

Authentic Stance on Behavioral Change

The third quality that the mindful clinician should develop over the course of his or her practice is an authentic view on behavioral change. This need for authenticity contraindicates one aspect of taking a problem-solving attitude toward the client to the extreme. That is, if a clinician believes the client must change her or his behaviors in order for therapy to be successful, and thus takes action during therapy to align with such a belief (e.g., by gearing interventions toward client change before the client is ready or willing), the therapist will no doubt face an impasse with the client. Holding the stance that the client must change, or thinking that you as the therapist hold the locus of control for the client, is not only counter to a mindfulness model but also aligns the therapist with most, if not all, the systems that attempt to strip the adolescent client of his or her autonomy (e.g., parents, teachers, probation officers, etc.). A mindfulness model of therapy supports the client's own autonomy and guides the client along the path of *authentic choicefulness*, or an increased ability to make choices based upon authentic feeling rather than quick reaction (I discuss this issue in detail in Chapter 4).

The above three qualities of authenticity, an intention for human connection, and an authentic stance on behavioral change all contribute to developing and maintaining the necessary atmosphere for an authentic relationship to arise and for effective therapy to take place. This can only occur within a therapist dedicated to practicing and harnessing such qualities.

A Philosophical Paradigm of Mindfulness in Therapy

One of the least referenced applications of mindfulness in therapy involves the philosophical assumptions that underlie a mindfulness model. A mindfulness model's philosophical foundations guide many aspects of the actual practice. These foundations lay the framework for assessment, case conceptualization, treatment planning, and intervention. I find the underlying philosophy to be most useful for case conceptualization about clients because, once I have a clear understanding of the core issues my clients struggle with, I begin to develop areas of emphasis that guide the treatment path.

As mentioned above, I adhere to an ontology that is heavily influenced by both Buddhism and existentialism, and, in accord with the lineage of existential therapists, I choose to define my ontology (to pay homage to, in my opinion, one of the best therapists this world has ever seen) through what Bugental (1965) classifies as "givens of awareness" (p. 65), namely, the core issues that high-risk adolescents struggle with on both an internal, intra-psychic level, and a conscious, explicit level. I do not contend that my view of the philosophical foundations of a mindfulness model is complete. By all means, as therapists and human beings, we can only view the world through our own lens and the following lens description is representative of my experience. It is my hope that future publications emphasize other philosophical assumptions that I have either missed or with which I do not align. Thus, the ontology that influences my work includes four givens of awareness that I have seen to be central to the lives of my high-risk adolescent clients: (1) human relationships, (2) suffering and tragedy, (3) choicefulness, and (4) change.

Human Relationships

The first major given of this model is that what's necessary for true growth in the client is an authentic human relationship between the therapist and the client. From an authentic relationship, the therapist can listen with compassion, challenge when necessary, have both positive countertransference and negative countertransference, and model a healthy adult–adolescent relationship; something that represents a dire need for most high-risk adolescent clients.

Human relationships permeate high-risk adolescents' experience. They not only are charged with negotiating an oftentimes rather stressful relationship with their parents or caregivers as they strive for independence but also need to develop and maintain peer relationships, which for most adolescents, supersedes their familial relationships (at least to an extent). That is, on the one hand, they are adamantly trying to connect with and define themselves in relation to their peer group (which in some circumstances manifests as joining a gang), and on the other hand striving for independence from the core family unit. For some theorists (Bugental, 1965, 1999; May, 1969; Yalom, 1980), a core concern of the human condition is the oscillation between feeling connected with the rest of humanity and feeling socially isolated. I have no doubt that this concern is as real for adolescents as it is for any population. Human relationships (whether family or peer group, strained or cohesive) can be a great source of anxiety, frustration, and the feeling of the unknown; all of which can be explored deeply with the client. I explore the different relationships within my clients' lives, along with our therapeutic relationship, as an avenue to facilitate growth and change.

Case Example: Joshua

Joshua was a 17-year-old male who, at the time of our treatment series, was incarcerated at the local detention facility. His home had been in a small apartment with his mother and his mother's sister's family (mom, dad, and two kids). He'd moved around with his mother his whole life, and, although they often argued, he felt a deep connection to her. Joshua was a high-ranking gang member of the prominent gang in his community, but expressed a desire to leave the gang to go to college and study music production.

Early in our relationship, Joshua expressed an interest in learning the necessary communication skills to speak with his mother during tense times without getting into a full-fledged argument. He disclosed that he felt disappointed in himself that he'd often argue with her, because he wanted to maintain the closeness in their relationship but also needed more autonomy. In working with Joshua on these communication skills, it became evident that he was experiencing a much deeper struggle than mere communication issues:

Joshua: I was in that gang awareness class the other day and we were talking about who would I choose, my family or the gang first? I was like, "I'm choosing my family first." That's what everybody says, even the down ass gangsters. Then the teacher was like, "Oh, so let's say you're walking down the street with your mom and your little cousin and you see a homie getting jumped by rival gangsters, what would you do?" So I was like, "I would've told my mom and little cousin to run back to the house, and then go help the homie." The teacher was like, "That's putting your family in danger, and choosing the gang first." I was like, damn! I guess I do choose the gang first. But I hella want to choose my family first! [*Shakes his head and looks down as he says this.*]

Himelstein: Joshua, what was it like for you to say that out loud? What's happening for you after saying you'd choose the gang over your family?

Joshua: [*Looks at me intensely and begins to tear up*] I feel like an asshole! [*Shaking his head left to right, looking down*] I ain't never said that out loud.

The above interaction led to a deep exploration of Joshua's desire to "put family first." In the course of our relationship, we explored his authentic feelings of wanting to rectify his relationship with his mother while at the same time feeling a need for further autonomy and independence from her. We worked collaboratively and often used our relationship as a source for discussing his relating style in general and with his mother. Joshua ultimately came to a place in his growth where he could speak authentically about wanting to be independent without an onslaught of guilt. Furthermore, Joshua began using his relationship with his mother as a motivator to confront his issues of needing respect and power from his gang member peers.

The fact that human relationship is a critical and underlying foundation of work with high-risk adolescents also extends to the therapist–client relationship. That is, not only will core themes of relationships arise within the story of the adolescent client, but the relationship between the adolescent client and adult therapist will be a critical factor in the entire process of therapy. For this reason, the philosophical given that human relationships play an integral role in the lives of high-risk adolescents will be both a content-level area of exploration in therapy and a process-level engagement between the therapist and client. I elaborate on this in depth in the next chapter.

Suffering and Tragedy

The second given of awareness of this model is that suffering exists in this world on a continuum from the mildest dissatisfaction to extreme tragedy.

For example, you might work with an adolescent client who is heartbroken because her boyfriend just broke up with her after a 2-week relationship. She will be upset and look to you (or others in her life) for guidance on getting through the break up. You might also encounter a client whose boyfriend was an active gang member and killed over the weekend. Both are examples of the existence of suffering and both require some response from you as the therapist. From the perspective of this model, your job isn't to try and eradicate your client's suffering—to tell him or her something along the lines of "It will all be okay," but rather to bring your response from the viewpoint of your own acceptance that suffering is a truth of the human condition. That girl who lost her boyfriend to gang violence is not going to be okay, at least in the short term, and it's important to honor the severity of that experience. What you can do, along with listening with compassion and supportiveness, is to begin to guide your client to form some meaning out of the experience.

High-risk adolescents are no strangers to tragedy. In a study conducted on trauma symptoms in incarcerated youth, Steiner, Garcia, and Matthews (1997) found that incarcerated youth are twice as likely to witness aggressive acts of violence (including murder) than are their non-incarcerated counterparts. The abundance of substance abuse, family discord, and economic issues that haunt the lives of high-risk adolescents make any attempts at eliminating suffering futile. Thus, when such issues do arise, I have found the models that confront suffering head on (e.g., Frankl, 1959) the most useful for creating meaning.

Case Example: Brian

Brian was a 15-year-old male and had been raised in a socio-economic class below the poverty line. I first met Brian at the outpatient substance abuse clinic where I work, and we began individual therapy. Our therapy was short-term, lasting approximately 3 months, after which he wasn't mandated (by his probation officer) to partake in therapy. Despite a relatively short term of therapy, I felt our relationship to be very strong. I felt comfortable with him as a human being, and he engaged my existential, present-moment style of therapy. Brian often presented in therapy with issues of death, murder, and stress. He often verbalized severe distress related to his home life.

After Brian left the clinic, 2 months passed with no contact. I then received a phone call with information that Brian had been re-incarcerated, had just been released, had been mandated by his probation officer to seek some sort of therapy, and would only talk to me. We then continued our therapeutic relationship. I quickly learned that the events that led to his incarceration had included acting out after another close friend was murdered due to street violence. This was the second friend in 6 months whom Brian had lost to street violence. He was undoubtedly in the midst of a hardening worldview:

Himelstein: I was really concerned to hear you went back to jail.
Brian: Man! Boy! That was some dumb shit!
Himelstein: You lost another friend.
Brian: I'm tired of this shit. Man, and my other homie just got caught in a murder case. He's gone for life!
Himelstein: I'm so sorry . . . so sorry [*At this moment I'm feeling an immense amount of compassion.*]
Brian: Can't nobody do nothing about this! This is just it! This is the game! Nothing you say is gonna help me! [*tearing up.*]
Himelstein: I know. [*I'm tearing up too.*] All I know right now, Brian, is that I'm extremely concerned for you. You seem like you're in a "fuck it" mood, and I don't want to hear about you ending up dead or in prison for the rest of your life because of it.
Brian: [*Tears flowing freely down his face*] I just don't get why God would do this to me.

What came of this interaction was a deeper exploration into his belief in God and a continual examination of how his worldview was being impacted from all the death and loss in his life. We collaborated on potential reasons for why he might be witnessing so much violence and often directly discussed his reason for living. It was through this exploration of his suffering, rather than an attempt to eliminate it (because neither of us had that power), that Brian began to make meaning out of his life experiences. We came to a point in our treatment in which Brian contextualized his experience through his own meaning and personal growth. He often would say, "I'm surviving this, I'm getting stronger," to signify that it wasn't his fault that such horrible experiences happened to him. His traumatic symptoms that were present immediately following the crisis (re-experiencing symptoms) began to dissipate.

Choicefulness

The third given of this model is that high-risk adolescents (let alone most human beings) have the ability to choose how to respond to their experience. A gang member from a broken and impoverished home may not have been able to choose the family, neighborhood, or economic status he was born into, but he can, with training, learn to choose how to respond to his mental, emotional, physical, and external experience. This a particularly important point not to misunderstand: the trouble high-risk adolescents find themselves in is not due solely to internal personal factors that have nothing to do with the context (neighborhood, poverty, etc.) in which they abide. On the contrary, this model holds an assumption that adolescents can increase their self-awareness to become more aware of the contextual and personal factors that influence their behavior and develop the ability to choose how to respond to them.

Issues of choice can be directly explored during the therapeutic conversation, enhanced by formal training (e.g., mindfulness), and can be assessed on a continuum from choosing to abstain or engage in certain behavior (external choices), to responding to internal experiences such as strong emotions (internal responsiveness). I often find myself contemplating my clients and asking, "How does the client relate to the idea that she can gain true power through choice?" From this assessment I emphasize different issues related to choice (formal training in choicefulness, direct conversational exploration, exploration of lack of responsibility).

Case Example: Joshua

Let's return to the case of Joshua, the 17-year-old gang member who was struggling with feeling connected to his mother while at the same time striving for independence from her. Joshua's largest amount of growth came from our conversations about the intersection between his relationship with his mother and choice. This started with an initial direct exploration of the concept of true power:

Himelstein: Joshua, what is it that draws you to the gang life so much?

Joshua: I just, everybody knows me. You know? I just like being known by everyone, respected.

Himelstein: You like the respect you get from the other gang members?

Joshua: Yeah. I feel . . . power.

Himelstein: Do you think it's true power you're feeling?

Joshua: I know it's not. I know they just respect me for the dirt (gang involved activity) I do.

Himelstein: Yeah I don't think it's true power either. For me, I really believe true power comes from within.

Joshua: [*Nods his head in agreement.*]

From the above initial conversation about true power, Joshua and I began exploring his relationship with the power he felt from the gang life, his yearning to leave the gang behind and make his mother happy, and his struggle between the two:

Joshua: I really want to leave this shit (the gang) behind. But every time I'm out there kicking it, even if I'm with homies who ain't in the gang, I just get in that mentality again. I'm just like, "Am I gonna make it?"

Himelstein: I admire your honesty with that. Most of the young men that come in here just tell me that they're going to change, and I know they believe they will, but I also know it's so much harder than that.

Joshua: Yeah. I just want to put my family first, you know?

Himelstein: Yes I do hear you. And I hear how hard that will be for you.

As Joshua and I continued this exploration over the course of many sessions, we kept returning to the theme that Joshua was going to use his relationship with this mother to overcome the gang life:

Joshua: [*At the start of one session*] I've made the decision to leave the gang life behind. I was standing at the fork in the road; the gang was down one path, and my mom down the other. I'm choosing my mom [*he says with emotion and the slightest tearing of the eyes*].

Himelstein: You've made that choice?

Joshua: Yeah!

Himelstein: [*I say with emotion/concern*] Are you prepared to make that choice every day?

Joshua: [*Nods head up and down, understanding that he will be confronted with this choice often*] It will be hard, but I'm dedicated.

Joshua began to understand that the choice he was making would be difficult and would confront him often in life. He understood that, on the one hand, he had made a huge choice to leave the gang, and on the other hand, he would be confronted by and have to remake that same choice very often to maintain his goal of a healthy and loving relationship with his mother. Joshua left treatment with me with a strong understanding of how his own choicefulness fueled a feeling of power uncurbed by anything other than his own sense of personal security. When I last heard of him he was maintaining a stable job, had a stronger relationship with his mother, and was not involved in gang activity.

Change

The fourth assumption of this model is the given that everything, from our emotional and subjective states, to our attitudes and thoughts, to our bodies themselves, will ultimately change. This is consistent with the Theravadan Buddhist belief of *annica*, which means impermanence in the ancient Pali language and is explicitly contemplated in various forms by practitioners. I remember listening to a talk by Joseph Goldstein, a prominent mindfulness teacher, in which he discussed the concept of Anicca. The basic premise of his discussion was that you could ask any hot dog vendor on the streets of New York, "Do things change?" And every one of them would say, "Of course, everything changes," implying that this given of awareness is nothing esoteric but rather an everyday experience common to humanity.

The given of change also uniquely touches the lives of high-risk adolescents because the adolescent life stage is full of change; the literal changes of their bodies, the sensitivity of their peer and familial relationships, their worldviews, and as mentioned above, for high-risk adolescents, the experience of death of friends and family. Change can be a source of suffering or an avenue for growth and the explicit exploration of a client's relationship to constant change lends itself toward the latter.

Case Example: Brian

Let's return to the case of Brian I present above, the 15-year-old who was re-incarcerated after a friend was murdered. The most obvious aspect of change or impermanence he was dealing with was death. He was consistently being presented with experiences of death (family members, friends, etc.). However, Brian also had a number of other experiences that pointed toward the given of change. Through our exploration of his experiences I began to gently nudge our conversations in this direction:

Brian: Man! Another friend got locked up (incarcerated).

Himelstein: I'm sorry to hear that.

Brian: Yeah, you know it's like I just feel like all my homies are either gettin' killed or locked up. It's like all my boys from growing up aren't around anymore.

Himelstein: It really seems like a lot has been changing for you over the past number of months.

Brian: Yeah. A lot of shit.

After a number of sessions with me mentioning the issue of change, Brian himself began to take a more active role in the contemplation of this given of awareness:

Brian: You know I've been thinking a lot about how everything around me is always changing. My friends are getting locked up or killed, my grandparents are dying. This shit can be intense.

Himelstein: Tell me more about how everything is changing.

Brian: It's like, I'm changing every day. It's easier for me to see how my thoughts change, how my emotions change. Even right now, this is gonna change. You're not gonna be here forever. We're gonna stop this at some point.

Himelstein: That's very true.

Brian began to come to his own insight that everything changes. It was from there on that our work focused on the immense loss he experienced and making meaning out of it. When ambivalence would arise, I would explore it with Brian and guide him to contemplate the meaning of his experiences, the moment, our relationship, and his life. I have no doubt that it was Brian's own self-determination that brought him to the doorstep of such insights and that such character would take him far in life. Brian and I completed our therapy relationship approximately 6 months later, and, the last I heard of him, he had moved to another state and started a family, which, for a person in his predicament, was a big success.

CONCLUSION

As has been illustrated in the above case stories, there is a strong potential benefit to incorporating mindfulness into clinical work on multiple levels. In my experience I have used mindfulness in four main areas: as a mindfulness-based intervention, therapist mindfulness, to contextualize the process (inter-subjective) level, and philosophically to case-conceptualize and guide treatment. Because of its absence in the literature, I presented in this chapter four philosophical foundations (areas from which to conceptualize) of a mindfulness model of therapy as they relate to working with high-risk adolescents: human relationships (e.g., how is the client relating to you as the therapist; his family; his friends; the rest of humanity), suffering and tragedy (e.g., the unfortunate truth that high-risk adolescents tend to witness more traumatic events), choice (e.g., the ability to choose how to respond to one's experience), and change (e.g., how one deals with change). For the sake of clarity, I reiterate here that these four aspects of awareness have been essential in my conceptualization of my adolescent clients. I am not stating these to be the only philosophical foundations of a mindfulness or adolescent process model, but rather sharing my experience of these as key areas requiring awareness in working with this challenging but rewarding population.

Further, it is important to note that most high-risk adolescent clients' issues will be able to be conceptualized within one (or more) of these philosophical categories. That is, there is no need to attempt to conceptualize one client as exhibiting issues in all four categories if he or she does not have major issues relating to more than one. Conversely, there is no reason to limit a client's presenting issues to one philosophical category when they clearly relate to more than one (e.g., both the case examples above were conceptualized on within two givens). On the one hand, I contend that all human beings deal with the above categories of awareness in some way in their lives. On the other hand, all clients present with unique features, and it is important to cater the model to them rather than to proceed the other way around. I urge that, when reading transcripts and conceptualizations throughout this book, the reader attempt to maintain an awareness of these foundational aspects of a mindfulness model of therapy and to think about how they might be deepened.

2

Building an Authentic
Relationship

One of the most crucial elements of incorporating mindfulness into clinical work with high-risk adolescents is the fostering of the development of an authentic therapeutic relationship. As I mentioned in the previous chapter, literature on mindfulness and therapy has overwhelmingly focused on teaching clients mindfulness as a technique to alleviate stress and other problems. Only a few publications (Hick & Bien, 2008; Safran & Muran, 2000; Surrey, 2005) have specifically addressed how the therapeutic relationship contributes to an atmosphere in which mindfulness interventions (or any intervention, for that matter) can be actively engaged. I view the therapeutic relationship as a vessel within which client growth occurs and strongly contend that my own awareness and intentions regarding the authentic human connection lay the framework for client receptiveness. Therefore, I believe that, as our community of mindfulness-based therapists continues to grow, we must lobby for the idea that the therapeutic relationship plays a significant factor in treatment.

Toward the end of my graduate studies, I was asked to attend a conference on psychotherapy for the "future" of our practice. One of the more interesting presentations was a researcher's meta-analysis regarding the agents of change in therapy (i.e., the actual components within therapy that facilitate change). Before presenting his findings, he decided to do an experiment on the audience (which was filled with approximately 150 licensed clinical psychologists). He told the group that he was going to make three statements about the effectiveness of different components of therapy and that, after each statement, if there were members of the audience who agreed with the statement, they should raise their hands.

After getting acknowledgement from the audience about instructions, he made the first statement: "Raise your hand if you think that the most effective treatments in psychotherapy are *cognitive- and behavioral-based* treatments." Of the 150 licensed psychologists, only two raised their hands. His second statement was "Okay, raise your hand if you think the most effective treatments are *empirically-supported* and *evidence-based* treatments." Again, out of 150, only two psychologists raised their hands. Finally he stated: "Now, raise your hand if you think that the psycho-therapy relationship and alliance produce the best outcome for clients." Almost everyone (excluding the people who had raised their hands earlier) raised their hands. After this exercise, the presenter went on to review his results which indicated what actually was effective for psychotherapy outcome (the relationship being one of many factors).

The psychologists in the audience probably weren't reminiscing on a rolodex of relevant research articles as they responded to this presenter. They probably were thinking, as I was, of personal experiences of seeing the relationship have a healing aspect in the therapy room alongside an intuitive sense that, at least on some level, outcome in therapy was predicted by the quality of the therapeutic relationship. In this evidence-based, quantitatively focused age of therapy it is sometimes difficult for those of us from the client-centered, humanistic, existential, and other process-based orientations to support our work's effectiveness. There has been a longstanding dispute between the relationship-based (non-manual-ized) and manualized approaches: On the relational side, we suggest that mechanical and manualized approaches to therapy do not take into account the uniqueness of each individual client and that, because they are manualized treatments, they are extremely easy to research and measure and, therefore, produce mostly positive results on those bases in the literature. On the other hand, therapists and researchers drawn more to manualized interventions argue that, with relationship-based therapies, researchers don't actually know whether and how they are effective and rely too heavily on uncontrolled variables.

This dispute, similar to that over qualitative and quantitative research, is far from resolved; however, some light has been shed on the role of the therapeutic relationship in regard to treatment outcome with adolescents. We are no longer limited in our advocacy of relationship's effect to referencing our intuition and personal experiences (although both the American Psychological Association (APA) and the Institute of Medicine recognize these aspects as influencing clinical expertise and client preference, which are two of the three components of evidence-based practice). A number of studies have investigated the impact of the therapeutic relationship on therapy with adolescents.

THE THERAPEUTIC RELATIONSHIP WITH ADOLESCENTS: CURRENT STATE OF THE RESEARCH

To spare you a detailed research report (as it is probably not the reason you bought this book), I will briefly summarize two *meta-analyses* on the topic. A meta-analysis is a particular quantitative research method that synthesizes the results of other research articles (on the same topic) and produces effect sizes regarding the independent variable (i.e., generates a statistical representation of the effect of the variable being studied—in this case, the therapeutic relationship).

The first of these meta-analyses was conducted by Shirk and Karver (2003), from the University of Denver, who were adamant about contributing to the literature on the effect of the therapeutic relationship with adolescents, something that has been thoroughly researched with adults (for a review, see Horvath & Symonds, 1991; Martin, Graske, & Davis, 2000) and much less explored with children and adolescents. Shirk and Karver selected 23 studies (18 peer-reviewed articles and five doctoral dissertations) that included a quantifiable method for measuring the therapeutic relationship and generated an overall sample size of $N = 1891$.

Results of this meta-analysis indicated that in fact the therapeutic relationship did have a modest, but consistent, impact on treatment outcome with child and adolescent clients (Shirk & Karver, 2003). This suggests that the relationship we build with our adolescent clients does have a positive effect on therapy outcome and that we should, therefore, hone our relationship-building skills in order to enhance this aspect of treatment. Another interesting finding of Shirk and Karver's was that, for children and adolescents with primarily *externalizing* symptoms, that is, "acting out" rather than "acting in" behaviors that are a staple of the presenting behaviors of the high-risk adolescent clients I speak of in this book, the therapeutic relationship was more strongly associated with treatment outcome. In other words, the role of the therapeutic relationship was found to be more strongly associated with positive outcome in adolescents who externally misbehaved and acted out. This finding further solidifies the importance and skillfulness that should be associated with building an effective relationship, given the difficulty in forming a relationship and alliance with youth who have predominately externalizing symptoms (Henggeler, Schoenwald, Borduin, Rowland, & Cunningham, 2009) and who are often labeled as "high-risk adolescents." For those of us working with this population, it is indicated that we must pay attention and be mindful of developing a quality therapy relationship.

This research study (Shirk & Karver, 2003) isn't, however, free from limitation or controversy. Indeed, one of the biggest issues when conducting a meta-analysis is to find a large number of studies that used the same measurement protocols to examine their construct, and most do not. Furthermore, the exact parameters of what the therapy relationship entails is unclear and debatable, a consideration that the second meta-analysis I review attempts to circumvent. In this more recent study, McLeod (2011) distinguished the "alliance" observed within the framework of Bordin's (1979) work as the bond (emotional aspects of client–therapist relationship), task (agreement and participation in therapy interventions), and goals (agreement of treatment goals), an element of meta-analysis that hadn't been clearly defined in the aforementioned Shirk and Karver (2003) study. McLeod (2011) included 38 studies (31 peer-reviewed articles and seven dissertations) and did not report a total number of participants, but it is safe to assume that it was large. Interestingly, this study yielded a much smaller effect size ($r = .14$) than did the Shirk and Karver (2003) study, suggesting that the therapeutic alliance does have an impact on outcome, though perhaps not as great an effect as the previous study had reported.

However, data on a number of participant variables were also collected in order to examine whether or not these moderated the association of the therapeutic alliance with treatment outcome, and, again, participants with externalizing and mixed (combining externalizing, internalizing, and substance abuse) symptoms had significantly higher effect sizes (externalizing: $r = .22$; mixed: $r = .24$) than did participants with both internalizing and substance abuse symptoms alone. This finding suggests that the therapeutic relationship has more of an impact of positive outcome on youth with these symptoms (i.e., high-risk youth).

Additionally, as our research advances, we may find even larger effects. McLeod (2011) chose to contextualize the therapeutic alliance within Bordin's (1979) definition. When we consider his definition of task: agreement and participation in therapy activities, it is clear that those participants in the studies McLeod synthesized that did not produce highly positive results on this construct (i.e., were treatment-resistant) may have had lower scores that reduced the size of the group's overall outcome. We have not seen any data indicating how therapists respond to treatment-resistant youth, and this response, I contend, is an integral piece of authentic relationship-building (something I elaborate on in Chapter 3). Therefore, we need further research and must be critical of how terms such as "relationship" and "alliance" are defined for measurement.

I view the therapeutic relationship as the intra and inter-personal dynamics that arise in both the subjective and intersubjective space between my clients and me. This includes how we feel about each other, dealing with resistance, confrontation, and exploration, along with any other experience that may arise within the vessel of therapy as a result of our relating to one another. For this reason, a key aspect of how mindfulness relates to the development of an authentic relationship is the ability to be mindful of, have intention for, and take specific action when different variables of the relationship unearth themselves in the present moment. To that end, I now turn to the intricacies of developing and maintaining an authentic relationship with high-risk adolescents. Such work includes clarifying from the outset (and subsequently if necessary) one's expectations of the relationship and becoming aware of and working within the four relational spheres I describe below.

THE FIRST ENCOUNTER: CLARIFYING RELATIONSHIP EXPECTATIONS

Time and again what I have seen to be extremely important is giving my clients an expectation of what the therapy process will encompass. This is helpful because, oftentimes, adolescents will walk into your office who have either never been in therapy before or have had negative experiences at treatment programs that have been counterproductive by being punishment-based. For this reason, I always discuss with my clients the process of therapy, which is so often misunderstood. It is often reflective of what is evidenced in the exchange below:

Himelstein: I was hoping we could take a moment and I could explain to you how I like to work, so that you could understand where I'm coming from. Is that okay with you?

Client: Yeah that's okay.

Himelstein: Cool, thanks. I just wanted to let you know that I see my job as creating an authentic connection with you. I'm not here to change you. I'm not here to judge you. My goal is really to get to know you and, if you're open to it, help you increase your self-awareness so that you can make choices in your life you won't regret. That means that in these early stages we can really do what feels right to get to know each other; we can talk about what you want to talk about, or we can play cards or another board game. It doesn't have to all be about what you were sent here for. Is that okay with you?

Client: Yeah that sounds good.

Himelstein: Great! It will take some time for us to get to know each other, but my goal is that, when you feel comfortable enough, you'll be able to talk about personal things with me and trust me.

Client: Okay, yeah, we'll see.

In the typical interaction above I give my client a clear description of the beginning stages of therapy, and, if you read closely, you noticed that I literally disclosed to my client the three therapist qualities I mentioned in the previous chapter as imperative to working with this population: authenticity, an intention to connect on a human-being level, and my stance on behavioral change. I find their explicit incorporation in the initial session to be very helpful in educating the client on the process of therapy. The above exchange is closer to the typical experience I have when first meeting clients, but I've seen everything from great appreciation (verbalized and or observable in facial expressions), to the slightest nod of approval, to indifference. The major point is that you are giving the client a summary of what she or he can expect in therapy, and this I consider to be a courteous and respectful opening.

Alongside giving expectations to your client, there will probably be a time at which you will have to do something similar with their parents or another third party referrer (attorney, probation officer, etc.). Parents who do not understand this type of therapy especially think they will be able to drop their son or daughter off with you each week, and 10–20 sessions later their child will be "cured" from his or her problems. It is essential to psycho-educate parents about the process of therapy. In this way, they will have the choice to either listen to your expertise (and have expectations grounded in reality), or choose to seek treatment elsewhere. I educate in a similar fashion parents and other third-party referrers (mostly probation officers) about how I work and the way I speak with my clients; I make sure to disclose my philosophy regarding the therapeutic relationship and to give them a loose timeframe based on my experience.

From the first encounter with new clients, I make sure to pay particular attention to how they respond to my explanation of therapy and determine whether further clarification is necessary. With some clients I have had to continually reiterate my philosophy of therapy over many sessions, simply because they didn't yet either trust or believe me because they were so used to more directive forms of treatment. In any instance, it is important to clarify your stance on the expectations of therapy whenever a client presents in a way that seems inconsistent with the philosophy. Through such clarifications, you can find yourself at the doorstep of the multiple avenues in which the therapeutic relationship reveals itself in session, in the moment.

FOUR SPHERES OF RELATING

What I review next are the components of an authentic adolescent–adult relationship. These include building initial rapport, deep listening and compassionate witnessing, skillful self-disclosure, and maintaining healthy and consistent boundaries. I like to think of these components as relationship *spheres*, or different vessels and interactive styles that can be delved into and out of in no particular order. Therefore, although I present these spheres in a particular order that seems to be the common progression of a therapist–adolescent client relationship (and I have experienced it this way a number of times), it is important to understand that such spheres are nonlinear, do not take a particular order, and can be activated at any time during the course of the relationship.

Sphere 1: Building Initial Rapport

Most therapists would agree that, whether working with high-risk adolescents or highly motivated adult clients, initial rapport-building is a necessary step to progress in therapy. This is even more essential with high-risk adolescent clients, given that oftentimes they are mandated to therapy against their will and walk in the office door with built-in negative associations about treatment. Because of this, I believe that every therapist working with high-risk adolescents, whether she or he focuses explicitly on the relationship or lends it minimal attention, should explicitly adopt a goal of building initial rapport and document it accordingly in her or his treatment plans. This solidifies the intention and gives the therapist some accountability for having an explicit intention to connect with the client on an authentic level. This is not only good practice but relieves the therapist of feeling as though something *needs* to happen in those first few therapy sessions.

Most therapists I train are both surprised and excited when I say that the most important, although not always the easiest, thing to do when building initial rapport with high-risk adolescents is to simply be yourself. As I stated in the previous chapter, authenticity is the foundation of an authentic therapist–client interaction. Still, therapists often get into problem-solving mode and feel that they need to "do something," or "fix something," during the first few sessions, so that they feel needed or useful. One of my closest mentors, the late Dr. Charlotte Lewis, a Transpersonal/Analytic/Jungian master clinician, always taught us to "get out of the way" of our clients, especially in the beginning stages of therapy. What she meant was that the client was a self-actualizing organism and that oftentimes it was our own need as therapists to fix, help, problem-solve, and so forth, that was a barrier to an authentic therapist–client interaction.

In my own practice, I have seen wonderful results from this resolve to get out of the client's way. As I stated in the previous chapter, if you walk into the therapy session with an agenda for why your client is already wrong and needs to change, you will align yourself with every system that is already against your client (court, parents, teachers, etc.). Thus, it is important to "get out of the way" in the initial rapport-building stages in order to engage the client authentically. This can actually take considerable effort and an honest dose of therapist mindfulness engaged by asking oneself, "Am I supporting this process or getting in the way of it with what I'm doing right now?" Such questions and their intentional response form the base for building initial rapport.

Beginner's mind

At this point you might be asking yourself what the therapy actually looks like in these initial rapport-building stages. This is where authentic curiosity contributes to the relationship. In these early stages I like to think of myself as practicing *beginner's mind*, being curious and open to the experience of each moment, a concept brought forth by the great Zen master Shunryu Suzuki (1998). I focus on my client's experience and am curious about him or her as an individual. I ask detailed questions about the client's experiences and life. I find that, like most other human beings, they appreciate being interested in. It helps to remember that this is different from prying or trying to get them to talk about something they don't want to talk about. I let them guide the conversation content and pace. You might find yourself in a situation in which your client simply doesn't want to talk. This is normal, and it is important not to be attached to a particular idea of therapy with new clients (i.e., that they should be talking). It is important to consider their experience: they are most likely in therapy against their will and probably have no idea who you are. Would you talk to you in that situation? Extensive discussion actually isn't necessary (at least for some of the time) when building rapport. If you find yourself in this situation, take out a board game (e.g., chess, checkers,) or deck of cards, and just drop the therapy spiel and try to relate to them on a purely authentic level. The early sessions provide a time to get a sense for him or her as a human being.

Sphere 2: Deep Listening and the Compassionate Witness

As you progress through building rapport with your clients, something quite amazing will begin to happen. They will begin to feel comfortable talking with you about their lives, and your relationship will blossom with trust. This trusting atmosphere is further developed by your skills as a deep listener. In this next sphere of relationship-building your client will lean in more with her story and experiences. She will expect you to take responsibility and be her "therapist," not just a "friend" who plays cards with her. Thich Nhat Hanh, the famous Vietnamese Zen monk who runs Plum Village in France, is often quoted from his lectures on *deep listening*. Deep listening is a type of listening done with one's whole being, not just the prefrontal cortex/executive attention part of your brain. When done in the presence of a client who is suffering, it is the base from which authentic compassion and true concern can arise. I remember listening to one of my clients, Eddie, a 17-year-old referred to me at the outpatient clinic, discuss his experience crossing the U.S. border:

Himelstein: Eddie, I get the sense from our conversations that you've really been through a lot.

Eddie: Yeah man. I been through so much!

Himelstein: What comes to mind when you say that?

Eddie: Crossing the border . . . [*pauses and leans head forward, his voice softening*] . . . crossing the border when I was 9 years old.

Himelstein: Tell me as much as you feel comfortable with.

Eddie: [*Pauses and begins to tear up*] When I was nine, me and my mom and two brothers crossed the border. We came here because my mom thought it would be a better life. We walked for 3 days through the desert; hiding in the day sometimes, sleeping in the cold at night. I had blisters on my feet, I was hungry, I was depressed. I didn't understand what we were doing, I just didn't want to be there. One time we got stopped by the patrol and we were all arrested. Then we came back and did it again, crossing the border and this time we made it. It was the worst few days in my life.

I listened with my ears, eyes, whole body, and heart. I remember being on the verge of tears and reflecting to myself later that evening and feeling that it had been the first time I had felt real compassion, authentic compassion, for one of my clients. It was out of this deep, mindful listening I accessed that Eddie began to observe my efforts to connect with him and truly witness his experience from a compassionate standpoint. What began to blossom was an ancient archetypal relationship: the sacred adolescent–adult relationship that many cultures have known, when children burgeon into adulthood. The authenticity, compassion, and trust in our relationship grew thick in moments such as the above interaction, where mindfulness of our dynamic guided my intentional interventions to unearth his awareness of the relationship, as well. After another interaction in which Eddie disclosed to me a severe and traumatic experience, I decided to go one step further and disclose the compassion I felt:

Himelstein: I'm so sorry to hear that Eddie.

Eddie: It's all good.

Himelstein: I really don't think it is. It brings up a lot of sadness in me, that you had to go through such traumatic experiences. I feel compassion for you right now because I care about you, and it's sad to hear that those things happened to such a good guy like you.

Eddie: Uh, thanks man.

Himelstein: What's that like for you Eddie, to have me, your therapist, tell you that I care about you and feel compassion for you?

Eddie: It feels good. Thank you. It feels like someone is out there for me, someone cares about me. I never really felt that from anyone besides my mom before, so I appreciate it. I trust you.

Himelstein: That's right, I do care, and I'm glad you trust me.

In the above exchange, I take the next step and unearth my feelings of compassion in order to explore how they affect Eddie. By doing so, I observed that we further solidified our relationship in our joint awareness, in existence. Eddie disclosed to me many times over the course of our treatment how thankful he was for my simply listening to him. We ended our treatment after about 6 months, and, the last I heard, he was holding a stable job.

Of course, not every client of mine responds in that same manner as Eddie did when I disclosed my feelings toward him or her. Indeed, when I inquire about my clients' experiences in such situations (when I ask how it makes them feel that I care), I at times hear responses such as "I don't know, kind of weird," and "it makes me feel a little funny." This is completely okay, and more of the norm than was Eddie's response, because a lot of high-risk adolescents do not have the self-awareness and verbal skills to describe their experience in such a situation. But the fact that they are feeling something points toward the idea that your relationship is having an effect in some way, as a result of your deep listening and compassionate witnessing. This is the power of deep listening. On the one hand, you as the therapist are not doing much. You are not interfering with their story, not trying to fix some problem they have. You are simply witnessing, simply being in full experience with them in the moment. On the other hand you are doing so much, because it takes a commitment to listen deeply with compassion, to turn off the voice in your head that tells you to fix the client's problem or jump in and speak. Such practice permeates a mindfulness model of therapy. It is my experience that it is in the times when we as therapists sensitively acknowledge our clients and let them know we are there, listening and fully present, that our disclosures have the potential to impact their lives.

Sphere 3: Skillful Self-Disclosure

As I alluded to above, compassionate and deep witnessing of the client's story can bring us to the doorstep of self-disclosure. This is an extremely important issue when working with high-risk adolescents; when done correctly, it has the potential to contribute to an authentic relationship; when done unskillfully, it has the potential to create a therapeutic impasse. Accordingly, the third relational sphere I present is that of skillful self-disclosure.

The idea of self-disclosure, especially with adolescents, makes most clinicians I train cringe. They often think, "Well, if I tell them this, they're going to want to know that, and that, and next thing I know they're going to know everything about me." The fact of the matter is that it is important, and at times essential, to self-disclose with adolescent clients. Consider their position: they are often forced into therapy with an adult whom they don't know and whom they probably think will try to change them. If there is any chance of creating an authentic relationship or building an atmosphere of trust, they must know that the therapist is a human being, not a mechanical machine attempting to fix their "problem." They need to know that the therapist makes mistakes and has preferences, just as does anyone else. Self-disclosure with adolescents humanizes the therapist—reveals him or her as a human being rather than simply another adult telling them that what they are doing is in some way wrong. Most clinicians who work with adolescents know that simply getting them to talk and engage therapy is a magnificent feat.

Clinicians often fear that, once they are put in a position to self-disclose, their adolescent client will in some way use whatever information was disclosed against them. In my experience it has been quite the opposite. When I'm in therapy with one of my clients and I'm put in a position to self-disclose, it is usually of auxiliary purposes to their story. Once I'm done disclosing, they immediately return to their story. It is as if, after disclosing in some detail their experience, they pause, extend their awareness outward toward you, and in some way ask for your input. They try to include you! Moreover, if a therapist were to attempt to deflect a direct question from a client because uncomfortable thoughts and feelings arise ("Oh shit, I really don't want to talk about that, how do I get out of this one?"), therapeutic impasse might occur. Consider a situation in which a client asks a therapist a direct question and the following occurs:

Client: Yeah man, I just been thinking about college and stuff, if I really want to go . . .
Therapist: Yeah.
Client: Did you go to college?
Therapist: I did.
Client: Where'd you go? Was it fun? I bet you got with hella girls.
Therapist: I think we should examine why you're so interested in me right now.

Above, the therapist completely dismisses the client's curiosity and employs the traditional "let's examine why you're so interested in me" deflection. This technique is not a negative technique in and of itself. It stems from analysis, and I only contend that it is often misused. That is, when called upon to self-disclose in some way, therapists often employ this response when they feel anxiety or discomfort, and that is a misuse. Not only could this statement be received with confusion and annoyance, but the meta-communication being transmitted to the client is, "I don't feel comfortable telling you that information and I don't feel comfortable being honest enough with you to say I don't feel comfortable telling you that information." To employ such a technique could aggravate the relationship with the client. It can completely derail the flow of the conversation and will probably leave the client thinking something like, "Who the hell is this person? He can't even answer my questions directly. Why would I ever trust him?"

There is, of course, no guarantee, but, as I mentioned above, your brief self-disclosure in the context of your client's story will further prompt him or her back into his or her own story. And sometimes this will lead to a fruitful conversation. In the example below, John, a 17-year-old client I had been working with at the juvenile detention camp, asked me about my college experience at one month into our relationship. Rather than deflecting, I entertained his questions authentically:

John:	Yeah man, I just been thinking about college and stuff, if I really want to go . . .
Himelstein:	Yeah.
John:	Did you go to college?
Himelstein:	I did.
John:	Where'd you go? Was it fun? I bet you got with hella girls.
Himelstein:	I went to UCSC, and it was fun and hard work.
John:	What about the girls?
Himelstein:	There's a lot of girls in college, usually about half of the people.
John:	Oh yeah?
Himelstein:	Yeah!
John:	Yeah, I mean I'm really just thinking about college. A side of me wants to go, but another side is like, "I don't know if I can leave the streets."
Himelstein:	It seems like you're torn between the college life and the street life. Is that true?
John:	Yeah.
Himelstein:	Say more about these two different paths.

In this interaction, John deferred from his story for a moment and called upon my self-disclosure, then went back to his story, which led to a fruitful explanation of his ambivalence between a life of academia and the life he knew: the streets.

Of course, you may not feel comfortable with certain situations/topics and need to honor your intuition and style. Be aware, however, that, if you don't feel comfortable disclosing anything at all, because of who you are or because of the orientation you've been trained in, you will hit relational barriers with high-risk adolescent clients. In order for them to feel part of something larger (such as the therapeutic relationship) they at times need to be met in that vulnerability, they need to know that you're there for them and can relate, even if by means of empathy and not personal experience. It is for this reason I contend that self-disclosure is not only an essential ingredient of the authentic adult–adolescent relationship, but is itself a practice that needs to be mastered and skillfully employed. Indeed, if, after reading the above transcript, you had a thought such as "Okay, but what about those clients that don't ask easy surface questions? What about those clients who really challenge you?," you are fair in your assessment of the incompleteness of the discussion regarding this issue thus far. It is important to briefly review different types of self-disclosure prior to discussing skillful self-disclosure.

Types of Self-Disclosure

Irving Yalom, the great existential psychotherapist and another of my literary mentors, describes self-disclosure as "not a single entity, but a cluster of behaviors" (Yalom, 2002, p. 83). He emphasized that self-disclosure from the therapist could be comprised of three aspects: mechanisms of therapy, here-and-now feelings, and the personal life of the therapist. Disclosing the mechanisms of therapy include discussing with your client the process of therapy (as I discussed above in regard to the first encounter with clients), the specifics of how you work, and potentially your theoretical orientation. Here-and-now feelings include the authentic, present-moment feelings you feel toward your client in response to his or her story or presentation. For example, a client may disclose something that makes you feel closer to him, or may be quiet and prompt the feeling of distance in you. Finally, you have the ability to disclose personal aspects of your life, from menial preferences (e.g., weather preference) to relatable experiences you and the client share (e.g., being incarcerated as adolescents). What is most important is that you use self-disclosure, in whichever of the above categories the disclosure may lie within, for the purpose of and in the best interest of the client. It should never be done outside of the bounds of self-awareness, and for this reason I refer to it as *skillful*.

Skillful Self-Disclosure

Skillful self-disclosure contains a number of important principles. It involves a high level of mindfulness and authentic self-awareness. To be skillful in disclosure, a therapist must contemplate the questions "How will this disclosure benefit the client?" and "Is this disclosure in the best interest of the client?," as well as "What is the reason I want to disclose right now?" By simply contemplating these questions, you position yourself in a mindful, self-aware, contemplative state from which you can speak mindfully and skillfully, and, if you choose, employ self-disclosure.

For example, when working with clients at the juvenile detention camp, I often find myself in the predicament of whether or not to disclose that I, too, as an adolescent, was incarcerated for a time. Before doing so, I always ask myself "Would it be beneficial for this client to know that I was incarcerated, too? Would this help the client to see me more as a relatable human being? Is this in this client's best interest? If so, how?" Then, if, after contemplating such questions, I believe the disclosure to be in the best interest of the client, I proceed. If, however, after contemplating the purpose of my potential disclosure, the uncomfortable thought and feeling of, "I want to tell him I was incarcerated, too, so that he likes me more," arises (i.e., a need to be liked that is yours and does not have to do with the client), I exercise extreme caution. In the latter situation, it would be unskillful and a misuse of self-disclosure to proceed to share, because I would be self-disclosing to satisfy a need within me rather than for the best interest of the client. A better approach when thoughts and feelings such as the above arise would be to disclose my present moment (e.g., "here-and-now") feelings of how I was feeling toward the client, a desire to relate. This exchange happened with one of my clients years ago —James, a 15-year-old at the juvenile detention camp that many other inmates revered and feared:

Himelstein: [*In a period of silence I thought to myself, "I should tell him that I was incarcerated, too. That will help build rapport. But is this in James's best interest? Am I just really trying to be liked right now? What is it that I am authentically feeling in this moment? Ah, his approval. I'm seeking some sort of approval."*]

Himelstein: James, I've just been thinking of the last few moments that for some reason I really want your approval. I view you as a tough dude, and I know a lot of the other inmates here seek your approval, too—they want to gain your respect and be liked by you. I found myself just now feeling the same way.

James: Oh yeah? Well, you know that's how it is here. I'm respected for certain reasons.

Himelstein: Yes, I know you have quite a reputation [*pause for about 30 seconds*]. James, I really believe that the reason I just felt that way is because I don't feel too close to you and I'd like to build more trust between us.

Above, I disclose to James my here-and-now feelings toward him: my need for approval. It turned out that James was very open to building more trust and that my brief, skillful disclosure led to fruitful explorations of his relationship with other inmates, his family members, and me. This all arose out of my contemplation of why I desired to disclose the initial material (that I was also incarcerated). In fact, in my entire relationship with James, I decided not to disclose that I had also been incarcerated, because I never deemed it to be in his best interest. With James, I barely disclosed anything about my life, because it didn't seem that it was necessary. The *personal-life-of-the-therapist level of disclosure* (Yalom, 2002) was not as much a part of my relationship with James as were my here-and-now feelings toward him in session. I have had many experiences with different clients where I have discussed my personal life, but only after I have deemed doing so to be in the best interest of the client. Thus, self-disclosure becomes a skillful means by which to connect, when it is used as a mindful intervention.

Of final note is the relationship between our own personal life experience and the degree to which we choose to share such information with our clients. Prior to sharing information about our lives there is another inquiry that must occur. We must ask ourselves whether we are projecting our experience onto the client. For example, if I have the thought, "I was incarcerated, so I know what it feels like for James to be incarcerated, and, therefore, I should disclose this with him to convey empathy," my self-disclosure has the potential to profoundly get ahead of itself. Can I really know James's experience? Can we, as therapists (or human beings, for that matter) really know another's experience? I believe the answer to be a strong no. We can only relate to experience, rather than fully knowing it. Even if the experience is objectively the same (e.g., being incarcerated) it does not necessarily mean it is wholly the same. For this reason, it is important to keep the beginner's mind of authentic curiosity with regard to our clients' experiences. This practice, along with questioning our own motives for self-disclosing, will empower us to, with full awareness, choose to disclose skillfully when the time is right. This solidifies our interventions in authenticity and empowers us to practice truly as mindful therapists.

Before concluding this section, I must add that you may have noticed that, in the above two transcripts, John and James are fairly open to my interventions and respond quite well. You again might be thinking, "But what about those clients that really pry? That really try and use our own self-disclosure to manipulate?" and, again, you would be making a fair assessment of the incompleteness of the issue. Accordingly, I now review one of the most difficult but potentially beneficial aspects of skill-ful self-disclosure with high-risk adolescents: maintaining healthy boundaries.

Sphere 4: Maintaining Healthy Boundaries

Skillful self-disclosure is interconnected with the issue of maintaining healthy adult–adolescent boundaries, because, when you do choose to disclose, even if done so skillfully, there is potential for the client to respond in such a way that calls upon great clinical skill and discernment. Or, a client might ask you a direct question, and you may feel it actually is inappropriate and choose not to disclose such information. It is the navigation of such sensitive interactions wherein skillful communication is necessary. This is why the final relational sphere I present is termed "maintaining healthy boundaries."

Maintaining healthy boundaries is a clinical skill necessary for any clinician working with high-risk adolescents; because some clients will try to pry, poke, and get information about you as either a way to get the conversation off them or for some other reason. This is a very real phenomenon and sometimes you do not even need to self-disclose to prompt it. Sometimes clients will simply want to use your life experience as a diversion from theirs. The more forthright you are in situations that call upon the maintenance of boundaries, the more you authentically explain your position of why you will not discuss information you are not comfortable discussing, the clearer your clients' expectations about therapy will be. With clear expectation, you can explain how firm bound-aries have to do with the sacredness and sanctity of the therapeutic relationship.

Let us consider a situation in which my own self-disclosure influenced a client of mine to directly challenge me. Shawn was 15 years old when I first started seeing him at the juvenile detention camp. He was a high-ranking gang member and I had been seeing him for less than a month when this interaction occurred:

Shawn: Yeah me and my girlfriend is having problems right now. I don't know if I can trust her on the outs you know? What about you? You got a girlfriend?

Himelstein: I do.

Shawn: What's she like?

Himelstein: She's great, I like her a lot.

Shawn: Oh yeah, I bet you slept with her last night huh? Did you get with her last night?

Himelstein: [*At this point, red flags arise in me, I don't feel comfortable sharing this information*] Shawn, I'm not comfortable sharing that with you.

Shawn: Aw what the? You want me to share all my stuff but you don't want to share yours?

Himelstein: It's not that I won't share stuff with you about my life, I did just tell you I have a girlfriend, but I don't feel comfortable talking about my sexual practices with my girlfriend. That's my personal business.

Shawn: It's all good, just tell me! I won't tell nobody, like that confidentiality we supposed to have.

Himelstein: I really just don't feel comfortable sharing that with you, Shawn. And I hope you can respect that.

Shawn: Come on man! I'm in here telling you about me. Just tell me what's up.

Himelstein: Shawn, even though this is a place where I hope we'll learn a lot about each other, there are going to be times that I don't think it's appropriate to share certain things with you. That's because I want to help you and sometimes boundaries need to be set up.

Shawn: That's bullshit. You just don't want to tell me.

Himelstein: It's not bullshit. You're right that I don't want to tell you about my sexual practices, but that's because I don't think it's relevant.

Shawn: I think you need to just tell me what's up so I can get to know you better!

Himelstein: Shawn, I'm feeling like you're challenging me right now. Is that true?

Shawn: What are you talking about?

Himelstein: I told you I wasn't going to tell you what you were asking about, but you kept on prying. I kind of have this sense that you were trying to punk (challenge) me in that moment. Do you think there's any truth to that?

Shawn: [*Contemplates the question for about 20 seconds*] Yeah I guess I'm just used to punkin' people into getting what I want. You know? That's how it is in here.

Himelstein: Thank you for being honest.

In the above interaction, I set a firm, but healthy boundary with Shawn. I used how I was feeling in the moment (mindfulness at the therapist level) to inform the therapy process and pick up on the meta-communication Shawn was sending to me (trying to challenge me and get his way). Shawn revealed, in that exchange, a large portion of information regarding how he relates to others in the world. This might have been missed if I had not engaged in any self-disclosure at all. This was, however, a unique situation in that this client had a high enough level of self-awareness to engage me in this interpersonal exploration. With other clients, I have experienced the setting and resetting of firm boundaries over the course of many sessions. It may very well be that the adolescents you work with are not mature enough or ready to engage you in such an authentic and responsible way. In these cases it is extremely important to not give in and compromise the sacredness of your relationship.

Maintaining healthy boundaries can be a difficult process, because some clients will distance themselves, in such an event. It takes a considerable amount of mindful self-awareness for a clinician in the above situation to breathe, examine how he or she is feeling, and then use that feeling to influence the course of therapy. This is why it is crucial for clinicians to commit to practicing mindfulness for the development of these skills (in all four of the relational spheres). Formal meditation is good for the development of mindfulness; however, when training clinicians, I urge them to make a formal intention to be aware of their own experience— thoughts, feelings, sensations—while conducting therapy and in relation to the client. This informal (but important) application of mindfulness will continually sharpen one's clinical skills and ability to set firm and fair boundaries.

CONCLUSION

It is important to take into consideration the nonlinear nature of the progression of a relationship with high-risk adolescents. In my experience, oftentimes, clients will come into my office and we'll spend weeks, if not months, in the early rapport-building stage. However, I have had the experience of clients being ready to express themselves and presenting as immediately strong candidates for therapy. This is because, even though many adolescents are mandated to therapy against their will, some still take advantage of it. They might not, at the outset, understand fully what the process of therapy entails; however, those who learn to understand that, at the base of this process is a sacred, confidential space in which trust, compassion, and acceptance arises—those that are suffering and either consciously or unconsciously organize toward authentic expression take advantage of this and speak their truth. For this reason, you may experience an adolescent client who comes into treatment and is ready to open his or her heart to you. There would be no need to brush this off and try to linearly go through the stages of early rapport-building before letting him or her express a personal, authentic self; you must meet the client where he or she is in the process. Alternatively, you might experience a client who comes into treatment and immediately challenges you to disclose information you are not comfortable disclosing. In this situation it would be important to clarify your personal boundary and educate the client on the process of therapy, again, meeting the client where he or she is in the process.

Thus, it is important to consider these "relational spheres" nonlinearly and as modes of relating the collective relationship that you and your client can delve into and out of in no particular order. These relational spheres are the specifics of the human-connection philosophical assumption I presented in the previous chapter; they have the potential to either motivate connection or create distance, and awareness and intentional processing of them unearths the here-and-now, present-moment, authentic state of the relationship. Awareness of the relationship is a practice, and clinicians should intentionally put forth effort to increase their skillful navigation of it. Thus, it is only in the best interest of the high-risk adolescents that the mindful clinician engages.

3

Working with Resistance

Working with high-risk adolescents can be an extremely rewarding line of work. However, working with this population is not always fun or easy. Do not underestimate that this can be a challenging and, at times, frustrating population to work with. Your definition of "successful therapy" may need to change when working with this population, given the resistance that may arise toward treatment. Therefore, an important aspect of successful clinical work with high-risk adolescents is the skillful navigation of client resistance as it arises. Moreover, because resistance is prompted by stimulus from the therapeutic context (i.e., being mandated to therapy, something a therapist says, an intervention a therapist attempts to employ), it should be viewed as a phenomenon that arises from the therapy relationship. For this reason I define resistance within the bounds of the therapeutic relationship and propose that its skillful use has much to do with the mindfulness of the therapist.

What I present in this chapter is a radical reframing of how we as therapists think of resistance. We first must expand our paradigm and define the truth underlying resistant behaviors. Once this is accomplished we must authentically examine our own role in the development of and our response to resistance from our adolescent clients. Finally, we must be skillful in our verbal and clinical responses when resistance does arise, in order to shed light on and explore with the client his or her underlying motivation for resisting.

WHAT IS RESISTANCE?

Oftentimes, resistance in therapy is viewed as something impeding client progress (e.g., see Miller & Rollnick, 2002). The presentation of resistance can take the form of silence, humor, aggression, challenging behavior, and a slew of other behavioral actions and states of mind. However, what all presentations have in common is that the client is implicitly (or explicitly) sending a message to the clinician that he or she is not in alignment with the current state of therapy. Moreover, simply having a goal to reduce resistance has limited efficacy. While, on the one hand, it opens the door of possible improved receptivity to therapy interventions, on the other hand, a large part of the process level represented in the resistance itself can be missed. That is, when resistance presents itself, it is both an inter and an intrapersonal action. The client is not becoming resistant for no reason. Resistance is arising because something in the context of therapy (i.e., an intervention the therapist employs, the therapist him or herself) has in some way touched an aspect of the client's psyche that he or she is not comfortable with, either consciously or unconsciously. Both the client's life experiences and present personality structure will influence how he or she will respond to certain therapeutic explorations (intrapersonal) and to the style of the therapist her or himself (interpersonal). For this reason, when resistance does arise, there is a strong opportunity to delve into the present tense of the therapist–client relationship and personality structure of the client to unearth her or his authentic motivation for resisting. This is where much therapeutic work can be done and authentic self-awareness can be heightened.

Of the psychotherapy sages whom I have never met but who have impacted my development through literature, Jim Bugental has probably most greatly influenced my work. Bugental (1999) suggests that human beings, either with awareness or lack thereof, will in some way walk through life with personal worldviews that will influence interpersonal styles of relating and "personality." Bugental (1999) compares what he calls the *self and world construct system* to *space suits*: just as, in outer space, a human being needs a space suit to enable her or him to breathe, to function, to survive, so it is that, in the social world, we need the self and world construct system, a system rooted in the ego that constitutes what is commonly viewed as personality. These construct systems make humans both unique in personality and conditioned in relating socially. When these systems face challenges, what Bugental terms *resistances*, or psychological defenses, arise. These mechanisms have the potential to both help and hinder human beings. Take, for example, a person who uses humor to deal with intense feelings of anxiety. When the anxiety becomes too intense, the defense of humor is triggered in order to challenge or resist such anxiety. In certain situations, this probably benefits the client and protects his ego. However, as he becomes conditioned to respond to anxiety with humor, there may be times when it does not serve him and when the resistance is blocking him from an authentic feeling that could be worked with (I elaborate on this with a case example below).

This is the deeper meaning and context from which resistance arises in the adolescent/adult interaction and, for purposes of clarity, I term them *resistance patterns*: the underlying psychological protective and hindering mechanisms that motivate the client's accessing of conscious and unconscious material that alert the defenses. It is in the holistic view that resistance patterns play an important role for our adolescent clients (and for every human being, for that matter) and should be welcomed, honored, engaged, and worked with. That is, resistance patterns are useful defense mechanisms that protect the ego from trauma and dissolution on the one hand and prevent authentic self-awareness on the other hand. In the mindful therapeutic practice, resistances are not pathologized, but rather recognized as systems in which insight and growth can occur.

THE GOLDEN BUDDHA

My favorite way to conceptualize resistance patterns is through a story that Jack Kornfield, the prominent meditation practitioner who has been a pioneer for Buddhism in Western society, writes in his book *The Wise Heart* (2008). He presents a story in which a monk in a Thai Buddhist monastery is cleaning his temple's meditation hall. In the back of the meditation hall sits a large, clay statue of the Buddha. The monk notices something shiny on the statue and, as his duties oblige, he walks over and attempts to clean it. The monk quickly realizes that the shiny object on the clay statue is actually underneath the clay, and on further inquiry, realizes that the clay is covering a solid gold statue of the Buddha. The monk learns from his elder that their ancestors covered the statue in clay to prevent it from being stolen by soldiers and pillagers. Essentially, the essence of the story is that the statue needed the rough, clay exterior in order to survive. Without it the statue would have been stolen and sold. And this is a wonderful metaphor for resistance patterns. They can protect us from trauma, pain, and other uncomfortable mind states (e.g., defend us from pain caused externally) and at the same time present as rough, ugly, and unattractive conditioned responses (e.g., shield us from our own motivation and authentic awareness).

In my work with the Mind Body Awareness (MBA) project, it is part of our curriculum to actually share this story with the incarcerated youth in our meditation groups. The reason for doing so is because this story suggests a very relatable metaphor for the incarcerated youth we work with: that we as human beings learn necessary defense mechanisms, coping mechanisms, and other skills in order to survive our context. Some of the youth we work with learn to be tough so that they don't get victimized, and others learn that any emotional expression outside of anger is viewed as weak, as a revelation of vulnerability. The major point here is that what we do (our actions, and sometimes our conditioned personality characteristics) are different from who we are at our cores. Incarcerated adolescents generally meet this discussion and metaphor with much appreciation and interest. It can literally have the power to disengage initial client resistance because it is holding the implicit stance of, "I know you've done some bad things in your life, but I also think there's more to you than the mistakes you've made, that you're a good person." When a clinician views resistance in this way, in such a way that positions the resistance as a part of the client's survival mode of being and as a potential for deeper connection, the probability of developing an authentic therapeutic atmosphere increases.

ADDRESSING RESISTANCE

In the above reframing of client resistance, my goal was to shift the traditional paradigm of resistance from thinking of it simply as something that needs to be eliminated for the client to progress to the evidencing of a rich process that can be worked with to unearth a client's authentic motivation. I now present a method with which to skillfully engage resistance in clients in session, first by becoming mindful of our own internal response to client resistance as therapists, and then by skillfully intervening with the client.

Therapist Mindfulness of Personal Response to Resistance

One of the reasons it is important to shift our paradigm on the concept of resistance is because it opens up our own hearts and minds as therapists to authentically become accountable for our own part in the interpersonal dynamic. If we take it as a given that resistance is both a hindering and a protective mechanism that comes from a deeper place and addresses the necessity of relating socially to the rest of the world, we, by default, are positioning ourselves within the resistant dynamic that arises within the client. The client is, in such moments, either consciously or not, protecting the self against something that we are doing, saying, or implying. Thus, in order to employ the paradigm of engaging resistance rather than trying to eliminate it, we first must examine how we respond to our clients' resistance.

In our response, we have the ability to be skillful and use the resistance to the benefit of each client. We also have the capability of becoming reactive and thus colluding with a client's interpersonal dynamic, which is something our own mindfulness practice can help us overcome. It is of utmost importance that therapists understand that, as their client's resistance is presented, their own resistance can arise and interact with their client's resistance to inform the presenting interpersonal dynamic between them both. This is why our own mindfulness of the response we as therapists have to client resistance, alongside our own resistance, is very important.

Therapist Response

Probably the most common initial experience I find myself having in response to client resistance is some form of anxiety or other uncomfortable feeling. I have found that most therapists I train concur with my experience, citing feelings of anxiety as the emotional state that arises in response to difficult client situations. This is a completely normal response and an aspect of being human. However, issues arise when therapists react hastily to their own anxiety in response to client resistance. It is before this occurs (reacting to personal anxiety), at the stage when anxious feelings first arise, that a commitment to mindfulness can provide therapists with a skillful avenue through which to manage their negative feelings.

Consider a situation in which a client comes into your office and, because of some therapeutic impasse, gets extremely upset and either yells at you or directly challenges you. What feelings do you think would arise in you? How would you then deal with such feelings? Your choice, or reaction, to your client, has the potential to have a great impact both in the moment of the relationship and on the larger process of therapy. If, for some reason, you react to your anxiety (and don't beat yourself up if this has happened—it will happen to everyone at some point because therapists are human beings and make mistakes), it might provoke further resistance. With Mikey, a 16-year-old with substantial substance dependence and anger issues whom I worked with early on in my career as a clinician, I learned that it was relatively easy for my personal response to his resistance to prompt further resistance on his part:

Himelstein: So, how's it going with you today?

Mikey: Good [*says abruptly and looks intensely at me for a number of moments*].

Himelstein: [*His look simply provokes some uncomfortable feelings in me; I feel the need to respond quickly and "do" something, and I react*] What do you mean, good?

Mikey: What do you mean, "What do I mean?" You know what the hell I'm talking about! I feel good! That's it! Why would you ask me a question like that when you know the answer! Man, I hate this shit!

In the above situation, I reacted quickly to my own uncomfortable feelings with the question, "What do you mean, good?" that then provoked Mikey to withdraw further into his own state of resistance. Not that such a question is inherently provoking; however, I believe it was the nature and tone of my question (the fact that it was a reaction and an attempt for me to in some form take control of the situation) that prompted further resistance within Mikey. Had I taken a moment to breathe, to center myself and be present to my authentic feelings in the moment, I would have had the chance to respond in a much more skillful manner. As Mikey's and my relationship progressed, I began reflecting on the feelings that would arise in me as a result of his resistance and made the commitment to practice my own mindfulness in session. This reworking of such responses proved effective, as in the interaction here:

Himelstein: How's it going today, Mikey?

Mikey: I don't want to be here!

Himelstein: Yes I get that sense.

Mikey: Why should I even trust you? I mean, you're just doing this as a job to get paid! You don't even care about me or any of these people you work with!

Himelstein: [*A number of uncomfortable feelings have arisen in me, including anxiety. I have just been directly challenged. My thought process is as follows: "Breathe, breathe . . . something is happening in me right now and, before I take action and verbalize anything, I need to get a hold on how I feel. I feel challenged. I'm also hurt that he feels that I don't care for him. Keep breathing. . . . Yes, I feel hurt right now, and that's what has usually caused me to react and 'do' something in the past." As I continued to breathe and was present to my emotional response and thought process, I decided it was time to verbalize my experience.*] Mikey, what comes up for me when you say that is a little hurt. It makes me feel hurt.

Mikey: Well, that's on you. I wasn't trying to make you feel that way but that's on you.

Himelstein: Yes I know. These feelings are my responsibility, but they speak to the fact that I do care and want to be here. I could easily be working somewhere else. I choose to come here because I care about working with you.

Mikey: I guess I never really thought of it like that.

In the above interaction, I breathe and become mindful of my present moment experience in response to Mikey's direct challenge. Rather than reacting and attempting to take control of the situation, which no doubt would have prompted further resistance, I owned my own feelings in the situation and spoke from a place of authenticity. I could have easily reacted and said something like, "Yes I do care!" very quickly, as a reaction, which could have prompted more resistance. Rather than reacting hastily, I took an inventory of my authentic feelings and spoke directly from my experience, conveying the "Yes I do care" from a place of calm responsiveness and authenticity. This skillful response to Mikey's resistance was premised entirely on my ability to become present in the moment and practice mindfulness. This proved very effective with Mikey, and our relationship progressed to the point where I could discuss with him how he was affecting me, how that related to how others perceived him, and what his motivation meanings under his anger were. When our treatment ended, Mikey had gotten himself a job, had a stable relationship with his girl-friend, and, when last I heard, ended up successfully completing his probation.

By committing ourselves to the explicit intention to be mindful therapists, we discover that the ability to manage uncomfortable feelings such as anxiety, rather than react to them, naturally increases.

The Use of Aikido

Being mindful to our own internal response is the base from which any skillful action toward our client proceeds. I learned early in my career working with high-risk adolescents that becoming mindful of what was happening inside me in response to client resistance was an important factor in successfully engaging this population. However, a question that routinely beckoned me was, "How, then, do I use this self-awareness in the best interest of the client—to move this process deeper into the moment?" I contemplated this and found my answer in the most un-assuming of places—a martial arts dojo.

In my graduate studies at the Institute of Transpersonal Psychology (now named Sofia University), all students had to take mandatory classes in aikido. Our school's co-founder, Dr. Robert Frager, alongside getting his graduate degree from Harvard, was one of the few Westerners in the world to be awarded a 7th degree black belt in the martial art known as aikido. Frager, known by my class and me, endearingly, as "Sensei Bob," would also teach us how aikido could be used in psychotherapy—not the physical practice of disarming one's opponent, but the interpersonal, mindful approach to dealing with aggression. Aikido was created by Morehei Ueishiba, known in the aikido world as "O" Sensei" (great master). He was a practitioner of many martial arts before he developed aikido, and a Shinto priest (a mystical spiritual tradition from Japan). The word *aikido* is broken down in Japanese to three characters: "*ai*," which means harmony, "*ki*," which means energy, and "*do*," which means the "way." Thus, aikido can be interpreted to be "the way of harmonizing energy." Of course, this is meant to be the harmonizing of what presents as inimical energies and the disarming of an attack.

As Sensei Bob transmitted these teachings and applied them to the therapy interaction, I began experimenting with that approach in my interactions with adolescents (at the time, I was a meditation teacher for the MBA project teaching mindfulness groups in juvenile hall) and found it to be quite helpful. It is similar to Miller and Rollnick's (2002) concept of *rolling with resistance*, which is a motivational interviewing technique that clinicians use to connect with clients, but it added one important piece I felt was missing in the rolling with resistance model: Although aikido is considered a "soft" or "internal" art, one must not misinterpret this as running away or letting the client walk all over you. What particularly drew me to this practice was that, rather than running away from an attack (i.e., just letting the client do whatever they please for the sake of not combating their resistance), aikido practitioners engage each attack, by using either circular or diagonal movements. Thus, rather than clashing head on (as with most martial arts), aikido uses the force of the opponent to harmonize with that energy. This was extremely useful to me in my experience at the time, because I knew that the last thing I could do in my meditation classes was to let the youth walk all over me. This would have been a misuse of the practice of aikido and an unskillful internal and external response to client resistance.

Let us consider a hypothetical situation in which a therapist simply surrenders to a client's resistance during the first encounter. The interaction could resemble something like the following:

Client: [*Says aggressively*] Yeah, so I really don't want to be here. This is stupid and I'm not about to do this therapy thing, so don't even try anything with me!

Therapist: [*Thinks to himself, "Okay, I should roll with this resistance and not combat it. I should just let the client be where he is; maybe we could just play cards—yes, that sounds good."*] Okay, why don't we just play cards?

Client: No!

Therapist: Okay.

Client: We're gonna do what I want to do in here. And, right now, that is nothing!

Therapist: [*Thinks to himself, "Okay, just roll with this. Do what he says."*] Okay we can do nothing.

Above, the therapist is attempting to roll with the client's resistance but is doing so in such a way that is setting the precedent for the client to continue walking all over him. He is not directly confronting the client, which may be necessary at the time; however, he is also not creating healthy boundaries. I have worked with many therapists who tell me that they attempt the above protocol, and it only results in a precedent of the client not respecting them. Thus, it is unskillful to retreat in such a fashion. A skillful response would have been for the therapist to engage, rather than retreat from, the client's resistance and develop a healthy boundary. If the therapist in the above scenario had maintained his center (i.e., had a firm stance and also rolled with the client's resistance), the outcome would be substantially different. Let's return to the interaction highlighting the internal experience of a skillful response to the client's resistance:

Client: [*Says aggressively*] Yeah, so I really don't want to be here. This is stupid and I'm not about to do this therapy thing, so don't even try anything with me!

Therapist: [*Thinks to himself, "Okay, breathe. This client's resistance is important. He is probably protecting himself from something. I can roll with this for now, but should maintain an awareness about if and how this will present again in the future."*] So what would you like to do?

Client: Nothing!

Therapist: Okay, how should we go about doing nothing?

Client: You know what I mean! We're gonna do what I want to do in here. And right now, that is nothing!

Therapist: [*Thinks to himself, "He is really resisting the idea of therapy and seems to want to control this interaction. I need to be sensitive to his current state while at the same creating a boundary over which he views me as a human being."*] I hear you. But I need you to understand that I'm a human being just like you. And even if you want to do nothing, my intention here isn't to hurt you or change you. It's just to respect you as a human being as I think you deserve. And I would like for you to at least attempt to respect me, as a human being.

In this scenario, the therapist still rolls with the client's resistance, but, rather than retreating from the negative energy from the client, the therapist both engages it and sets a healthy boundary. The therapist's internal process is extremely different than it was in the previous example: he breathes, turns towards the resistance rather than away from it, and understands when a necessary boundary should be raised. He doesn't attempt to simply roll with the resistance with the hope it reduces, but rather meets the resistance in the moment and views it as important data. Of course, the thought process I unpacked above may be more elaborate even than some of my own in similar interactions, but, with experience and intention, a therapist may experience the essence of that thought process in a feeling, intuition, or sensation. Nonetheless, this is a skillful example of harmonizing with a client's negative energy and laying the foundation for a relationship in which the resistance can be engaged. Such a skill takes experience and time to develop, but, once honed, is essential in meeting the resistance of clients in a compassionate and authentic way. To that end, it is necessary for the therapist to make a commitment to his or her own mindful path in order to raise personal awareness of his or her own responses to client resistance. From there, he or she may choose interventions on the verbal level to skillfully engage the multiple layers of client resistance.

WORKING WITH RESISTANCE PATTERNS

I now come to the point in this chapter of reviewing the process of working with and "through" resistance patterns. I have dedicated this portion of the chapter to the intricacies of approaching, on a verbal basis, a client's resistance. However, as I conveyed above, it is imperative to understand that the skillful verbal engagement of resistance depends entirely on the therapist's inner process and worldview. Whereas, in the above section, I focused on the therapist's inner process, here I present the nuts and bolts of engaging resistance externally with the client, with the internal process being implied.

Traditional Resistance

One of the most common forms of resistance from adolescents in therapy is simply not wanting to be there. Remember, most high-risk adolescents are mandated to therapy, and this positions you as the therapist against the adolescent (at least in his or her mind). Thus, it is oftentimes important to clarify and educate the client from the start about the particular way you'll be working with him or her. This is similar to what I presented in the previous chapter about the first session but expands on it in that it is essential to get some information out when the client initially presents in the relationship with resistance. For example, one of my clients, Vickie, a 17-year-old girl who was mandated to therapy from her probation officer, presented in our first session as below:

Himelstein: So what can I help you with in therapy?
Vickie: Nothing. I don't want to be here and I don't need to be.
Himelstein: Are you pissed off that you have to come here?
Vickie: Yeah! It's like I always have someone trying to tell me what to do or fix me or some shit!
Himelstein: Is that something you think I'm going to do too? To try and tell you what to do and fix you?

Above, just in the first few moments of our interaction I note that Vickie is angry about being in therapy because she's mandated, and I question her about whether or not she thinks I will be another who attempts to tell her what to do. In this moment, she was metacommunicating to me the implicit assumption that I would fit that criterion, so I engaged it immediately. The conversation continued:

Himelstein: Is that something you think I'm going to do, too? To try and tell you what to do and fix you?
Vickie: I mean, I guess so. I've been in therapy before and all my counselor did was tell me that everything I did was wrong. Isn't that your job?
Himelstein: Actually, no, it's not. I'm here to help you explore you. Explore your own self-awareness. Only if you want to. I'm not going to tell you what to do or try to change you.
Vickie: Yeah, well, I don't even really want to be here or talk to you.
Himelstein: That's okay. I can't force you to talk.
Vickie: Yeah, but I gotta be here. My probation officer will lock me up if I don't show up, and that sucks.

Himelstein: That's true, and I don't have any power over that. But I can tell you that, when you do show up, we can talk if you want, or not if you don't want to. If you want to play cards or a game, or talk about something totally unrelated to why you're supposed to be here, that's fine, too. I'll be here.

Vickie: [*Pauses for a moment to digest my response*] Hmm. Well, I've never gotten that response from a therapist before.

Above, I explore Vickie's initial resistance and, at the end of the interaction, her resistance is coupled with surprise and curiosity. This by no means took away Vickie's resistance to being in therapy, but it did work toward softening her initial rigid stance.

High-risk adolescents may present initially on a spectrum of resistance; from the more mild-mannered Vickie above who just didn't want to be in the room to the more confrontive types who believe that their entering into therapy is a direct attack on who they are. When this resistive adolescent walks into therapy, oftentimes, the anger, resentment, and resistance that were placed upon her or his mandater is transfered onto the therapist. For example, Wayne, a 15-year-old client I worked with in the juvenile detention camp, entered therapy already thinking my goal was to strip him of his personality and change him into a different person (something I'll elaborate on much more in the following chapter). Our first interaction went as follows:

Himelstein: How's it going with you today?

Wayne: All right I guess [*sucks his teeth and looks away*].

Himelstein: You just sucked your teeth and looked away after you told me how you feel. Is there something else you're feeling right now?

Wayne: I'm just not really into this therapy stuff. It's always, man, you know . . .

Himelstein: You've been in therapy before?

Wayne: Yeah.

Himelstein: And it sounds like you had some negative experiences?

Wayne: Yeah, I just don't like people always trying to change me! If they were from where I'm from they would understand that you can't change where you're from!

Himelstein: And it seems like right now you might be concerned that I'm going to try and change you, too. Is that right?

Wayne: Yeah! I mean, isn't that your job?

Himelstein: Actually no. It's not my job to change you, that's your job. If you want to change something about you, it's your choice. If not, that's also your choice. The way I do therapy is to connect with the person sitting in front of me and help that person develop more self-awareness. It's really up to them if they want to change or not. Do you think you might be open to that?

Wayne: So you're saying that you're not gonna try to change me? Not gonna try to tell me to stop smoking weed and hanging out on the block?

Himelstein: No. Like I said, that's not my job. Now, if you do want to change something about yourself so you stay out of jail, I'll help. And if you don't want to change anything, that's okay, too. I just want to get to know you and connect.

Wayne: Well, I guess we can try it out.

Above, I begin to unhinge Wayne's assumption that I am trying to change him. I clarify how I view my job and am transparent about my goals of the therapeutic process. This relaxes the initial tension that most mandated clients feel when entering the therapeutic relationship. It opens the possibility to work from an awareness-focused, rather than change-focused model of therapy. Further, it models a clarifying communicative process; oftentimes a corrective experience for high-risk adolescents who are used to being stripped of autonomy in interactions with adults. In Wayne's case, we needed to have this conversation quite a few times before he could trust that I actually was not trying to change him. Eventually, he began to trust me and we explored different aspects of his self-awareness. Some clients might need reassurances multiple times because they are not used to being approached this way. They are used to being pushed around by the system. If reassurance is needed multiple times, the therapist should continue to provide it and to differentiate him or herself from the system, as needed. Such a corrective experience builds trust in the relationship.

Resistance Patterns

To reiterate, while resistance can manifest in many forms and lie on a spectrum of traditional surface resistance to deep underlying motivation, resistance patterns, a subcategory of resistance, are the specific protective mechanisms (the *space suits*) that human beings employ to protect the ego in some way.

One of my close mentors, Dr. Myrtle Heery, who worked very closely with Jim Bugental, taught me that the goal of resistance work is to get the client to the point where, when a resistance pattern does arise, the client has the choice either to employ it (in order to protect the ego in some way) or to disengage it (to work with authentic underlying feelings). It is this "working through" of resistance that is the major feat when working with repetitive resistance patterns. The identification of and working with such patterns in the therapy session promotes growth by way of the client becoming more aware of his or her personality habits. Therefore, the skilled therapist encourages his or her client to explore how a particular resistance pattern serves him or her in the moment it occurs. Over time, it is the hope that the client attains further autonomy over these personal processes and engages the *actual*—the client's authentic, present-moment, subjective experience (Bugental, 1999).

Consider, for example, a situation in which your major resistance pattern was to use humor every time you felt anxious. If you had the ability to choose whether or not to employ this resistance pattern, if you actually had the ability to take a step back from your personality, you would have a considerable skill in self-awareness. Being able to undertake this process with an adolescent is no easy feat and doesn't always result in the skill just described. But it can be meaningful, and just becoming aware that such patterns exist takes the client far beyond termination of treatment.

Of course, much rapport is needed in order to engage a client about a particular resistance pattern, which is why I place such a heavy emphasis on relationship-building and the four relational spheres of an authentic relationship. Without the proper relational context, traditional resistance to therapy, or to you as the therapist, may arise in your clients. Thus, within the context of an authentic relationship, a steady progression through working with resistance proceeds as follows: identify the resistance (i.e., make sure it arises a number of times before thinking it an underlying resistance pattern), mention it to the client (i.e., bring up what you are noticing with a nonattacking, exploratory approach), name the pattern (i.e., when you have built rapport with the client around the resistance and the client accepts and understands, at least to an extent, the resistance pattern, find a phrase or way to identify it), and, finally, engage the client, using Socratic questioning as to how that resistance pattern serves him or her in that moment. This has been the general progression in my experience, but is by no means an absolute path. The path can be circular and nonlinear, depending on the client and how he or she presents the resistance pattern.

To exemplify the general progression, in the experience below with Maddox, a 16-year-old client I had been seeing for a number of months, after long observation and consideration of his resistance pattern, for the first time, I comment on it:

Maddox: Did you know Meoff?

Himelstein: Who?

Maddox: A former inmate here.

Himelstein: Oh, no I didn't.

Maddox: You didn't, for real, he said he knew you. His first name is Jack.

Himelstein: No I didn't know him.

Maddox: Jack . . . Meoff. Ha, ha, ha, I didn't get you. I get most people with that.

Himelstein: What is it that you were doing right there?

Maddox: I was trying to get you to say "Jack me off."

Himelstein: I noticed that, and I noticed you joke around a lot in our sessions.

Maddox: Yeah, you know, I like to joke around.

Himelstein: Do you really feel happy all those times when joking?

Maddox: I mean, uh, sometimes.

Himelstein: Sometimes? What about right now?

Maddox: I guess I feel depressed other times, it sucks up here being locked up.

With Maddox, I commented on what I believed to be a resistance pattern of humor, which I've seen often in incarcerated youth who present with large amounts of anxiety. Over a few sessions I kept exploring and redirecting Maddox's awareness to his process of resisting his true emotions in the moment. As Maddox's awareness of the resistance developed, I presented the idea of naming it for further observation:

Himelstein: What would you call that?
Maddox: What?
Himelstein: You know how we talked about how at times you joke around when you're really feeling depressed?
Maddox: Oh yeah.
Himelstein: Let's give it a name. What would you name it?
Maddox: Shit . . . umm . . . Playtime.
Himelstein: Playtime.

By Maddox naming his resistance pattern, I was able to continue to comment on it as it arose throughout our sessions. As Maddox's awareness of his resistance pattern grew, I began asking him about its function for him:

Himelstein: Are you doing playtime right now?
Maddox: Yeah.
Himelstein: How is that serving you right now?
Maddox: I don't know, what do you mean?
Himelstein: Well, what good does it do for you to be doing playtime right now?
Maddox: Oh yeah, I guess it helps me not to think of my depressed feelings being here locked up.
Himelstein: That seems to fit, but what I'm asking is, in this moment, how is it serving you to use playtime in our therapy session?

After challenging Maddox to contemplate how his resistance pattern serves him, I found that he began to become aware of it more in his daily life as it was occurring. The goal of this intervention is to encourage the client to explore his underlying and authentic feelings. This promotes an authentic engagement in the client's present moment experience.

The above illustration of the client employing the resistance technique of humor is an example of a client with considerable awareness and willingness to examine himself. In many cases clients may present with resistance patterns infused with anger, aggression, and hostility. It is important for therapists to maintain awareness that identifying and working with resistances take time. Time is needed to notice it arise more than once, time is needed to build rapport with the client about the particular subject, and time is needed to confront the client on how the resistance serves him or her. A therapist should exercise significant caution before attempting to label a resistance pattern. A therapist should always ask her or himself, "How is what I'm observing being filtered through my own biases?" before forming a definitive label or attempting to fit similar client experiences in an a priori defined category. Although I strongly believe that if you search deep enough, every human being needs protective resistance patterns, I also believe that there is no sense fishing for patterns in adolescents whose habits are still forming or who do not yet have the ego function to intelligently participate in this aspect of therapy. In such situations, the therapist should rely on other aspects of the relationship for the treatment path.

CONCLUSION

Finally, I conclude this chapter with the truth that the material presented here takes considerable time and effort to master. As therapists, we are all human beings, so there will be times when resistances and other relational dynamics have arisen, and, in reflection, we wish we had handled the situation more skillfully. Becoming aware of these dynamics as they arise is very difficult and is a practice in itself. Therefore, there is no sense in feeding the inner critic that contends there has been bad practice for those of us who need extra time, outside of the client interaction, in order to case-conceptualize before bridging such reflection within the moment's processing and intervention with clients. It is the deep intention to practice mindfulness in-session that has the potential to increase our ability to be mindful of our own anxiety, respond skillfully and blend with any resistance, and increase the awareness of both our own and our clients' resistance patterns. With substantial commitment and practice, we increase the ability to meet our client's authentic motivation underlying resistance and can engage the moment in authenticity.

4

The Paradox of Change

One of the most critical aspects of working with high-risk adolescents is the clinician's personal and theoretical view on *behavioral change*, or the explicit intention to change behaviors and attitudes. The push for behavioral change is often a charged topic, because it creates a power struggle: most high-risk adolescents either do not see a problem with their behavior and/or do not desire to change it, and most authority figures push, force, and attempt to get them to change their behaviors. As I mentioned in Chapter 1, clinicians can harness certain qualities to become proficient in effectively engaging this population (e.g., authenticity, an intention to connect on a human-being level, and a relaxed stance on behavioral change). The role of behavioral change, how it happens, and our influence as clinicians are all critical elements in the development of a successful therapeutic relationship. Additionally, because most high-risk adolescents are mandated clients (e.g., from parents, caregivers, the court, etc.), clinicians should expect to encounter frequently the issue of behavioral change (e.g., the effect of parents pushing, or legal system forcing, change).

Issues begin to arise when high-risk adolescent clients enter our offices and clash with our pre-existing schemas of how change and growth occur in therapy. In fact, most psychotherapy orientations assume that some form of change is necessary in order to effectively participate in therapy in a meaningful way. Thus, when we hold true to such assumptions, the interaction between our clients and ourselves can cause tension, therapeutic impasse, and a multitude of other potential problems.

Not all therapy orientations, however, assume that behavioral change is a necessary component to meaningful participation in session. According to Ingram (2006), existential therapists understand client change as the choices the client makes that may or may not be related to the "success" of the therapy. Rather, the primary concern in therapy is to help the client develop a greater self-awareness, an ability to engage in the authenticity of her or his subjective state, a capacity for exploration of a spiritual world-view, and an engagement in the therapist–client relationship (Ingram, 2006). For example, whether the client has another behavioral outburst, recidivates back into incarceration, or keeps engaging in prior risk-taking behaviors is not the primary concern of the existential clinician who works with high-risk adolescents. This is not to say that no attention or concern arises when such behaviors are ongoing. On the contrary, such behaviors may be an avenue by which to confront a client on issues of life and death, her or his resistance structure, or other fruitful issues. What I contend, in this chapter, is that a clinician who maintains a radical stance on behavioral change (e.g., that the primary concern of therapy isn't behavioral change but, rather, self-awareness) will ironically encounter less client resistance to change. This is the case, apparently, because, when clients are not forced to change their behaviors, it is more likely that they will be open to developing a relationship with their therapist and be more receptive to interventions.

Furthermore, the above approach to the development of self-awareness, rather than behavioral change, is in alignment with a mindfulness model of therapy. It would be safe to assume that one of the major goals of mindfulness practitioners is to assist in increasing some aspect of the client's self-awareness. Further, many mindfulness practices place a strong emphasis on acceptance, compassion, and not attempting to control things outside of one's control. To that end, maintaining a strained effort to change a client's behaviors (when he or she doesn't want to) creates a power struggle and puts the therapeutic relationship at risk for impasse.

The largest risk of attempting to force a client to change is that the therapist will be aligning him or herself with systems that the adolescent already loathes. Adolescents (especially high-risk adolescents) are well accustomed to receiving preaching, advice-giving, and top-down teaching from parents, teachers, probation officers, juvenile hall staff, judges, police officers, and even some treatment interventions (e.g., Alcoholics Anonymous). If you as the clinician employ such a position on behavioral change, you will align yourself with the aforementioned systems and take part in creating barriers to the clinician–client relationship. As I noted above, the irony in my personal experience has been that, because they were not forced to change, clients approached in a mindfulness model felt more open to the possibility of therapy and change. Let's reconsider the interaction I presented in the previous chapter in which I faced resistance with Wayne, my 15-year-old client:

Himelstein: How's it going with you today?

Wayne: All right I guess [*sucks his teeth and looks away*].

Himelstein: You just sucked your teeth and looked away after you told me how you feel. Is there something else you're feeling right now?

Wayne: I'm just not really into this therapy stuff. It's always, man, you know . . .

Himelstein: You've been in therapy before?

Wayne: Yeah.

Himelstein: And it sounds like you had some negative experiences?

Wayne: Yeah, I just don't like people always trying to change me. If they were from where I'm from they would understand that you can't change where you're from!

Himelstein: And it seems like right now you might be concerned that I'm going to try and change you, too. Is that right?

Wayne: Yeah! I mean, isn't that your job?

Himelstein: Actually no. It's not my job to change you, that's your job. If you want to change something about you, it's your choice. If not, that's also your choice. The way I do therapy is to connect with the person sitting in front of me and help that person develop more self-awareness. It's really up to them if they want to change or not. Do you think you might be open to that?

Wayne: So you're saying that you're not gonna try to change me? Not gonna try to tell me to stop smoking weed and hanging out on the block?

Himelstein: No. Like I said, that's not my job. Now, if you do want to change something about yourself so you stay out of jail, I'll help. And if you don't want to change anything that's okay, too. I just want to get to know you and connect.

Wayne: Well, I guess we can try it out.

As I suggested in the previous chapter, this is a common response most mandated clients offer when coming to therapy and is a form of resistance. If my responses are examined carefully, however, it is also apparent that I'm exercising my radical stance on behavioral change. I tell Wayne that it is not my job to change him, and, in stating that, send the implicit message, "You're not a bad person." Again, I clarify how I view my job and am transparent about my goals of the therapeutic process. This relaxes the initial tension that Wayne felt toward therapy.

In the mindfulness-based substance abuse treatment intervention I cofacilitate at the juvenile detention camp, the final session involves a focus group in which the whole group reflects on their positive and negative experiences in the former sessions, and anything they might change about the group for the next round of participants. I ask them a number of qualitative interview questions to obtain data to continually make the program better (something I'll elaborate on in Chapter 7) and, for the last question, I always ask a "catch-all" question to examine any other inform-ation I might have missed that would be valuable. This is the verbatim response that Rocket, one of the participants, offered:

Himelstein: Okay, the last question I want to ask you all is, is there anything else that I might have missed during this interview? Anything else you'd like to add about your experience in this program that I didn't specifically ask about?

Rocket: Yeah. I just wanted to say that I really appreciate you guys as teachers (facilitators). I liked how at the beginning of the group you told us you weren't trying to change us. Most of the staff here tell us what we do wrong and how we need to change. They don't get it that it's up to us if we want to change. Not them. I just wanted to give you a shout out because most therapists and teachers don't get that, and you guys do. It made me feel more open to hear what you had to say during these 8 weeks and be in this group without thinking something like "here goes some more bullshit I gotta listen to."

Motivational interviewers employ a similar stance on change, and preliminary research suggests its effectiveness in reducing drug use among different populations (Miller & Rollnick, 2002). Thus, it is no surprise that being relaxed about behavioral change has consistently arisen as a model preferred by clients in our focus groups, and my cofacilitator and I are preparing to publish these findings.

DISCLAIMERS OF THE RADICAL STANCE

To summarize the previous discussion, I contend that a radical shift in stance towards behavioral change as a goal of therapy is necessary in order to create authentic relationships with high-risk adolescents. If a traditional stance on behavioral change is upheld (i.e., having a strong belief that a client needs to change one or more of his or her behaviors), the therapist will indubitably align her or himself with a multitude of systems (e.g., parents, the court, probation officers, teachers, etc.) that the client views as oppressive, and a barrier to the relationship may rise. If, however, a radical stance is undertaken, that is, if the therapist is more concerned with the development of self-awareness than with behavioral change, the irony of the approach is that it creates conditions under which the client can change.

The effectiveness of this approach, however, is not without disclaim. It is imperative for clinicians to contemplate a number of disclaimers in order to conduct effective therapy. These disclaimers include addressing clients who wish to change some behavior, the motivation of the therapist employing the radical stance, and the confrontation of high-risk behaviors.

Disclaimer 1: What if a Client Wants to Change Something?

When I present these concepts at conferences, I always highlight three disclaimers regarding this stance on behavioral change, in order to put to rest any misconceptions. The first is relatively simple and regards dealing with clients who actually want to change something about themselves. As I mentioned above, high-risk adolescents are often averse to clinicians presenting them with a bunch of ways they "need" to change and interventions supporting that, because there is an implicit message in such an approach: Whether or not it's the intention of the clinician, the client often hears implicitly, "There's something wrong with you, something wrong with your personality, and it shows through the way you behave. We need to change you and your personality." Because of this metacommunication, clinicians often encounter much resistance. But that doesn't mean that if you don't take that approach (i.e., you do take the stance on behavioral change I present in these pages) your high-risk adolescents will never want to change something about themselves or want help alleviating some form of suffering. Consider how ridiculous the below hypothetical interaction would be:

Client: I've been stressing out over this test that's coming in a few weeks. Didn't you say that meditation could help with that type of stuff? Can we try that in here?

Therapist: Oh, actually my stance on change is that I don't believe in forcing it. So, in regard to changing your stress level, you're on your own.

If the above ever transpired, it would be absurd, let alone that it would produce the effect of your client feeling extremely shut down and dismissed. Of course, if a client wants help with some issue in his or her life (e.g., reducing stress), by all means, the clinician should help that client in the way it has been requested. There is no violation of this stance on behavioral change in such a case, because this stance only applies to working with clients who are particularly resistant to therapy. It is of the utmost importance that clinicians understand this concept.

Disclaimer 2: The Stance Must Be Authentic

Second, it is of extreme importance that the stance on behavioral change, when needed and implemented with those youth who are resistant, is an authentic stance. That is, a clinician should not merely shift his or her paradigm on change with resistant adolescents simply because the irony of that matter is that it will reduce resistance and greater change might actually occur. This stance cannot be used as a manipulation, because, metacommunicatively, this will be transmitted to your adolescent client, your relationship will lose authenticity, and you will be leaving yourself open to the risk of having the relationship completely break down.

Miller and Rollnick (2002) suggest that rolling with resistance is a method for helping reduce resistance and helping facilitate the client's advance to the next stage of change (motivational interviewing adheres to Prochaska and DiClemente's (1984) *transtheoretical stages of change*).

What I want to distinguish is that we must really believe that it is the choice of the client to change. This goes back to the philosophical foundation of a mindfulness-based model. The locus of control for choosing whether or not to change resides within, and only within, the client. To suggest that we as clinicians "make" or take absolute credit for a client's change is premature and unethical. We are guides, facilitators who help clients develop self-awareness, but it is ultimately the choice of the client to change and to be willing to encounter the hard work it usually encompasses. Thus, if a client comes into session with what Prochaska and DiClimente (1984) call the precontemplation stage (i.e., having no desire to change and possibly even denying a problem in the first place), it is not our place to employ the stance on behavioral change I suggest above simply because it has the potential for the client to progress to the next stage of change. If it is the client's choice to not change, that decision must be respected and honored by the clinician (in the next section, I review the significant difference between respecting a client's position on not wanting to change as opposed to the clinician's not caring for or colluding with the client's risk-taking behaviors).

Please do not misinterpret the above paragraph. My intention is not to suggest that motivational interviewing is in any way guilty of negligence or of being a "bad" form of therapy. On the contrary, there is much evidence to suggest that it is quite effective for adult substance abusers and mixed evidence in regard to its effectiveness with adolescents. My hope is that my philosophical stance on change, a mindfulness-based stance rooted in authentic locus of control, is more of a constructive critique that highly benefits clinicians working with high-risk adolescents.

Another quite important reason for why the stance must be authentic regards the current state of how we as a society view adolescents. Adolescence is a time in a person's life during which he or she is often striving very hard for autonomy. Nevertheless, unfortunately, at this stage of development they are told what to do and what not to do by so many adult figures: parents, teachers, police officers, probation officers, judges, and, sometimes, even clinicians. Thus, when a clinician employs instead this mindful stance on change authentically, a specific and different metacommunication is consistently being relayed to the high-risk adolescent: "You are your own man or woman; you have the power to make your own decisions, and I respect that." Of course, it is of utmost importance to be able to assess when a high-risk adolescent really does *not* have this capacity because of a mental health or developmental issue. I am not referring to these types of clients. I'm referring generally to high-risk adolescents whose autonomy is often shunned, neglected, and even, at times, laughed at in this society.

Finally, I believe it is important to clarify the idea of choicefulness and an internal locus of control versus the truth that sociological mechanisms do influence individual people (i.e., although we all have a capacity to choose, outer forces play a role in shaping that choice). For example, a client who was raised in an impoverished neighborhood did not choose to be raised in that impoverished neighborhood. The choices he may find himself taking on a daily basis differ significantly from those that present themselves to a young man who was not raised in that neighborhood. Because of this, some responsibility must be placed on the societal factors that underlie some of the choices he may make in his lifetime (e.g., to deal with poverty, he might sell drugs). Thus, these adolescents will at times engage in such activities for survival purposes, and I'm not suggesting in any way that, because someone has the power to choose to stay away from those activities, he or she will, or even should, do so. My point does not actually have to do with what choice the client does make (although, as I said before, it seems there is some irony in that this stance on change leaves the client more open for change), it is that authentically maintaining and conveying respect for your clients' autonomy and ability to make decisions will, more often than not, bring them closer to you and enhance trust in the relationship. From this platform, your client can choose, with full awareness, what action she or he might take in her or his life.

Disclaimer 3: Confronting High-Risk Behaviors through Authentic Concern

The third, and potentially most important, disclaimer regarding this stance on change is the distinction between, on the one hand, not holding concern for or not believing that the client's high-risk behaviors are dangerous (and thus not incorporating objectives and goals about such behaviors in the treatment plan) as opposed to, on the other hand, paying close attention to, being present with, and confronting her or him about such dangerous behaviors. Simply because one assumes the existential and mindful stance that change is the choice of the client does not by any means excuse the clinician from extending care toward or being concerned about the client's high-risk behaviors. Thus, if a client told me she was going to continue taking drugs to the point of overdose, I wouldn't think to myself, "Oh well, it's her choice. She can do what she pleases."

What is different in this model is the medium through which those high-risk behaviors are confronted. Rather than implicitly communicating "You're doing bad things and you need to stop," the mindfulness-based clinician uses the relationship to elicit deep concern and care for the client. For example, a client of mine, Michael, who was 16 years old at the time I met him, literally walked into my office and, within 5 minutes of the session, precipitated the following interaction:

Michael: Hey man. I know you're just here to do your job, but there's nothing wrong with me or what I do. I know selling drugs will get me locked up. I know holdin' heat [carrying guns] could get me killed or locked up for the rest of my life. But I'm a thug and that's me, so I got nothin' to get from you.

I had been briefed about this client's high-risk behaviors by a colleague and expected some form of resistance, but nothing that blatant. Of course, my response was akin to my responses in the previous chapters:

Himelstein: Hey, that's cool man. I'm not here to change you. That's really up to you. My job is just about getting to know you and helping you to become more self-aware, if you're open to it. We can really use this time to talk about whatever you want, play cards, whatever. We can even talk about football if you want.

Michael: Oh yeah, football! Yeah that's my sport right there.

As with most clients who have no intention of changing, Michael then relaxed his assault and strong position on therapy. Our course of therapy was slow, and we often related through the sphere of building initial rapport; I just let him guide the conversation and we talked about the topics he wanted to present, and sometimes nothing at all was said when we played cards. However, simply because I mainly traversed the initial rapport-building sphere did not mean that when he did talk about his high-risk weekend activities I couldn't confront him (and feel concern for him as a human being). As aforementioned, however, rather than scolding him, telling him what he was doing could get him in trouble or killed (of course he knew that), and aligning myself with those systems he'd spent so much time positioning himself against, I used our authentic relationship as a medium within which to confront him:

Himelstein: How was your weekend?

Michael: Cool, cool. Got into some real shit though this weekend. Man, I was out there grindin' (selling drugs) and some goons rolled up and we got into some beef (serious conflict). They started shooting at me and my homeboys and a few of us shot back and then we got the fuck out of there. Crazy shit, huh?

Himelstein: Yeah. That's real crazy. There's a chance that you wouldn't have been here for this session.

Michael: I know, I know.

Himelstein: Hey man, how long have we been seeing each other here? I'd say about 10 weeks right?

Michael: Yeah something like that, I think that's right.

Himelstein: You know, just getting to know you and talking about football and the other interests we have in common, I've really become fond of you. I think you have a lot of cool qualities, and, in this short time, I've grown to care about you. I'm really concerned for you, Michael. I'm really scared one day I'm going to walk in here for our session and I'm going to get a call telling me that you've been killed over the weekend, or killed someone else and are locked up.

Above, I'm using Michael's and my relationship as a platform to confront his behavior. I'm disclosing with him my authentic here-and-now feelings for him so that he can see how his behavior affects his environment (in this instance, me). What happened next was for both of us to process how he felt about my care for him: the types of thoughts and feelings that arose as a result of my self-disclosure. The session continued, after a minute or so of silence:

Himelstein: What's that like for you, to have your counselor tell you that he actually cares about you?

Michael: Well, I don't really know. It's kinda weird. I mean, thank you, but it's kinda weird.

With some clients, when we explore this dynamic, I at times get the response, "I really appreciate that. No one besides my mom has really told me that before," which is the main point in presenting that intervention, to show them that they are authentically cared about and concerned for. This response requires a client that has moderate to high self-awareness and is comfortable disclosing such information. Generally, however, I get the response that Michael gave above. However, that is still a response that can be used to facilitate the relationship and self-awareness in the client. Oftentimes, clients who rarely get told that they are cared for do not know how to respond and verbalize their feelings, so feeling "kinda weird" is a normal response. Our conversation continued:

Himelstein: Does it feel weird because not many people say stuff like that to you?

Michael: Yeah! I mean, yeah only a few people in my life really say they care about me.

Himelstein: Is it hard for you to trust someone who says that to you? Was it hard for you to trust me when I said that?

Michael: No. It's not like a lot of people say it and I don't believe them. They just don't say it.

Since Michael's and my relationship was strong, I felt comfortable disclosing my feelings toward him and exploring that topic. The conversation would come up every few sessions, whenever he'd report extremely high-risk behavior. And it was not as though I would always direct his awareness to me and my care for him as his therapist. Sometimes we would discuss his relationship with his mother:

Michael: Another gun fight this weekend. My boy actually got shot!

Himelstein: Oh shit! Is he okay?

Michael: Yeah, we took him to the hospital and he's gonna be all good.

Himelstein: Wow! That was a close call!

Michael: Sure was.

Himelstein: Man, you know how it scares me that you won't show up here one day. I feel really scared about that [*my heart rate was rising*].

Michael: I know man. I can't be doing stuff like that. I mean I still want to be a thug but it's like two gun fights in a month, that's too much for me.

Himelstein: Yeah man. And you know what I can't stop thinking about: If I feel this way about you, if I care this much about you just knowing you for this short time [at this time about 3 months], I can't even imagine how your mom must feel. How scared she'd be if she found out about all of this. How devastated she'd be if you were killed.

Michael: [*Pausing for about a minute, he averted his gaze from my eyes and began looking at his hands, with his head leaning forward*] Yeah [*voice softened*], I mean that would be all bad [*cracked voice holding back tears*].

This was evidently the first time Michael had really contemplated how his lifestyle could affect the one person in his life he loved the most, his mother. Our therapy sessions over the next few months consisted of discussing our shared interests (mostly football, given it was football season), playing cards and other games, and, when he did mention his risky behavior, the only intervention I used was the one above: I confronted his behaviors using our relationship and exploring his relationships with the people he loved in his life. I did all this without telling him not to engage in such behaviors. It was not that I told him I thought it was okay for him to be engaging in such behaviors. But when he did ask for my opinions, I made sure he understood that it was my opinion that he should not be doing what he was doing, not approaching it from the stance of my telling him not to do it. In our last session, Michael disclosed something with me that he said he had been contemplating during the prior few weeks:

Michael: You know man, I really been thinking. About all that stuff we been talking about in here. About my lifestyle. I'm thinking maybe I should keep it cool for a while. At least until I get off probation, I don't know if I'm gonna be kicking it on the block like that anymore.

This happened to be our last session, but it confirmed for me, in my heart, that the "stuff" we had talked about—the exploration into his relationship with his mother, the relationship with me—had at least prompted him to contemplate the context of his life. Of course, the researcher in me cannot confirm for sure that it was that intervention of confronting his behavior with my genuine concern, alluding to his mother's concern, and the processing of feelings that had arisen for him in those exchanges, that was the one thing that made him come in for that last session and say what he said to me. There would be too many variables to control in such a study. What I do know is that, each time we would explore his relationship to me, to his mother, to himself, he would take a few moments (sometimes minutes) and stay quiet, seemingly contemplating what we were discussing. I have also seen with many other clients the power of using the relationship to confront such behavior and to maintain the therapist–client alliance, which is ever so important when discussing change, growth, or anything, for that matter, with high-risk adolescents.

CONCLUSION

In sum, I have presented in this chapter my position on behavioral change: a therapist who employs a traditional stance toward change and believes that successful treatment entails behavioral change on the client's part will contribute to client resistance, while a therapist who takes a radical stance on behavioral change and focuses on the therapeutic relationship and the development of self-awareness will, ironically, create the conditions in which a client can, in turn, change. This radical stance on the therapist's part must be authentic and by no means denies the therapist the ability to be concerned for and confront a client's high-risk behaviors.

There is one final point, however, that I must convey in the closing of this chapter. The idea that having this stance on change, even if authentically, will work (i.e., create conditions for change that the client takes advantage of) all the time with every client is dishonest. Inevitably, there will be times when your client chooses not to change anything about him or herself and it will lead to tragedy. This is because this population is termed "high-risk" for a reason: they often get into serious trouble and engage in both self-harming and externalizing behaviors. This can have for them sad, and even tragic, results.

One of my clients with whom I did some particularly challenging, but good work was released from the juvenile camp and at first flourished while at home. He completed his electronic monitoring (house arrest) phase, and successfully completed about 6 months of probation without a re-offense (a particularly noteworthy achievement). I later was notified by the detention camp approximately one year after his release that he had been involved in the intervening period in two robberies, in one of which a victim had been shot, and in the other of which a victim was stabbed. He was arrested, and, as a legal adult, he was sentenced to state prison. He received a 25-year sentence. In a matter of one night, based on the decisions he had made, his life was now drastically changed in a negative way. When I heard of this, I felt an overwhelming amount of sadness: "This was a good kid," I thought, "and now his life is over!" If you work with this population long enough, you, too, will have tragic stories to share. Murder, suicide, overdose, prison; these are all things that have a very good chance of happening to some of your clients if you work primarily with this population. It is a truth that I cannot censure. It is hard, sad, and at times difficult to deal with.

However, it is the way in which we as clinicians view and deal with these tragedies that can either protect us from or cause us what is called vicarious trauma and compassion fatigue (developing our own symptoms and feeling extremely burned out). This is why I stress that a mindfulness model of therapy involves so much more than merely teaching mindfulness and meditation. A philosophical foundation of the principles of mindfulness has the ability to prompt a paradigm of self-care. If we cling too tightly to the outcome of our clients, if we take too much credit for their success and blame ourselves for their failures, we will inevitably prompt ourselves for suffering. It is for this reason that we must accept that there is suffering in this world—that good people have the potential to do evil things and that, sadly, it sometimes happens that they do.

What I am not suggesting is that you are not affected by a client tragedy. To respond in that way would negate your authentic care for your client. If a client commits suicide, gets murdered, overdoses, or suffers from some other tragic decision, it will be a sad day. Being sad and feeling compassion for your client and his or her family are normal responses to such tragedies. It is when you cannot sleep for weeks, and such events begin to inhibit your day-to-day functioning that you need to seek consultation and potentially to augment your practice by accepting in addition a different clientele. Remember, self-care is the most essential aspect of being a mindful therapist. Since we are the tools of our trade, we must care for ourselves in such a way as to reduce burnout, and, if it does occur, take appropriate action to facilitate our own healing. Otherwise, we would be doing our clients and ourselves a great disservice.

P A R T

CONTENT

5

Worldview and Spirituality

While the primary importance of successful work with high-risk adolescents relies on the work of the relationship and its many components (e.g., relationship spheres, resistance work, the paradox of change, process-level work), there are still important aspects of a mindfulness model of therapy that are best interwoven with the content level of therapy. I do not mean the particulars of explicitly teaching mindfulness to a client (this is something I will cover in Chapter 9), but instead refer here to the potential for using the underlying philosophy of a mindfulness model as a paradigmatic view of the content that a client presents in therapy.

For example, one of the gaps in the current literature on mindfulness-based interventions with almost every population is the measurement of insight- or epiphany-related experiences and realizations. It is almost entirely nonexistent (at least I haven't found any articles). The literature has focused on more easily measured phenomena such as stress, anxiety, and other similar constructs. This is not to say that the research is negative; in fact it's quite the opposite. However, the point I contend here is that, given that many mindfulness teachers often dub mindfulness as "insight" or "insight-oriented" forms of meditation (e.g., Kornfield, 2008) rather than concentrative forms of meditation, shouldn't we measure and explore the impact that such insights could have on our therapy clients and research participants? The reason I believe so strongly in the importance of gathering data about these particular results of mindful therapy is that I have seen firsthand the impact an insight can have on a client's life. I am not referring to times when I have taught clients meditation and, right after the session, they pop up emphatically and say, "I just had the biggest insight!" What I refer to is the explicit intention of a clinician to assist the client to develop self-awareness and the insights that arise on such a path. By simply having this intention with clients (of course you won't force them to have conversations they don't want to or are not ready for) you are opening the pathway for them to experience insight.

In my personal experience, and in the experience of an abundance of other mindfulness practitioners and teachers, insights broaden, deepen, expand, or change one's personal worldview in some fashion. As I suggested in Chapter 3, our worldview (e.g., what Bugental, 1999, calls the *self-and-world construct* and *space suits*) is an essential element of the practice of mindfulness: by practicing being aware of our own worldview, of our own stories we construct of reality, we gain further insight into the nature of the self. It follows that, because of this process, we, and our clients we hold this intention with, begin to relate to us and to deconstruct the mrigid and conforming views of reality that are most often blindly abided by.

Consider the following: a young adolescent male from an inner-city area continually witnesses death in some form or another (e.g., a friend is murdered, a grandfather dies from cancer, a distant neighbor is murdered). What is the cost of such experiences for the adolescent's psyche? Traditionally, at this time in life, this adolescent may be striving for independence and learning new ways of engaging with the world beyond the care-giving unit. He may be struggling with Erickson's (1980) *identity vs. role confusion* stage of development and merely beginning to strive to become aware of who he is as a human being, let alone what his purpose in life may be. What kind of a message is he getting from constant death around him? He may begin to believe the world is not a safe place, or that God either does not exist or is out to get him. The adolescent constantly surrounded by death grows into adulthood with a negative worldview and, therefore, may be psychologically compromised. This approach's overt attention to the client's worldview through the lenses of resistance patterns, spirituality, and other conceptual frameworks is yet another reason for its conduciveness to insights for high-risk adolescents. Present-moment awareness and interventions on the clinician's part bring greater awareness to the way in which the client relates to the outside world and lend themselves toward conversation and discussion that will bring about greater authentic self-awareness that facilitates insights, epiphanies, and the continual development of the worldview.

RESEARCH ON SPIRITUALITY IN ADOLESCENTS

Before delving into specific examples and case illustrations relevant to client worldview and how it relates to a mindfulness model of therapy, I believe it is important to review some recent research on the role of spirituality and well-being in adolescents. I have chosen to review this research because of the method's relationship to expanded worldviews and spirituality. That is, oftentimes adolescents who consider themselves spiritual discuss their spirituality not only in terms of God or a specific spiritual belief but also in reference to the worldview they hold toward greater humanity. Furthermore, in both of the studies that I review below, one of the dependent variables is existential well-being as measured by the Spiritual Well-Being Scale, an instrument that directly investigates worldview. The below studies shed light on and develop the argument that adolescents have the potential to embrace, and to benefit from, spirituality.

In one study, Davis, Kerr, and Kerpius (2003) investigated the relationship between meaning, purpose, spirituality, and anxiety in a sample of at-risk youth. Forty-five participants (25 female, 20 male) with ages ranging from 14 to 17 were recruited through a workshop targeting at-risk youth. Four measures were completed by attendees for research purposes: (1) the State and Trait Anxiety Inventory (one of the most commonly used anxiety measures in self-report research); (2) the Spiritual Well-Being Scale; (3) a revised version of the Allport–Ross Religious Orientation Scale; and (4) the Social Provisions Scale. The results showed that, for males, anxiety was inversely related to spirituality. That is, as scores became higher on the state and trait anxiety inventory (indicating higher levels of anxiety), spirituality (as measured by the spiritual well-being scale) was measured as being lower on the same continuum, and vice versa. No correlations were found to be significant for females; however, when Davis and colleagues examined more closely the extent to which trait anxiety could be accounted for by spirituality (i.e., how the belief of spirituality impacts anxiety), they found that results of the existential well-being subscale, a subscale of the spiritual well-being scale, were significant for both males and females.

Further, Davis and colleagues also used a statistical method called *backward regression* to examine whether or not the individual's reported level of existential well-being could predict that person's anxiety scores (regression is a statistical analysis one step deeper than correlation; it looks not only for significant relationships among variables, but at whether one variable can predict another variable) and found that a lack of existential well-being was a significant predictor of anxiety. What the above research suggests is that spirituality, more precisely existential well-being (feeling as though one has purpose in life, is content with life, etc.), significantly impacts the anxiety levels of the at-risk youth from the sample (i.e., whether those who have greater existential well-being have less anxiety).

In another similar study, Cotton, Larkin, Hoopes, Cromer, and Rosenthal (2005) examined the role of spirituality on depressive symptoms and health risk behaviors in a sample of 134 high-school students. Participants ranged in age from 14 to 18 and completed the Spiritual Well-Being Scale (as in the study above), the Children's Depression Inventory Short Form, the Youth Risk Behavior Survey, and two items measuring religiosity: "How important is religion in your life?" and "Do you believe in God/Higher Power?"

Cotton et al. (2005) conducted Person's r correlations and regression analyses (as similar to analyses used in the above study), and the most significant finding was that existential well-being and religious well-being (as measured by the Spiritual Well-Being Scale) accounted for 29 percent of the variability in depressive symptoms and 17 percent of the variability in risk-related behaviors. Further, existential well-being was the only significant predictor of depression and risk-taking behavior. What this means is that, again, research supports the idea that existential well-being (i.e., feeling content in life, feeling as though one has a purpose in life) plays a major role in mediating depression and risk-taking behaviors in this sample of adolescents in that it decreases the chances of either of these two states or activities occurring for an individual at that stage of life.

The underlying tenets from the findings of the above two studies is that spirituality, namely existential well-being, plays a significant role in the lives of adolescents. I further contend that spirituality broadly defined is an avenue into our high-risk adolescents' worldviews and can be engaged to produce greater self-awareness and, in turn, greater autonomy, choice, and, perhaps, growth by the client. I have no further intention of summarizing research in this chapter; however, if you wish to investigate the phenomenon further, I direct you to a meta-analysis on adolescent spirituality and mental health conducted by Wong, Rew, and Slaikeu (2006).

ADDRESSING WORLDVIEW

I have chosen to present here two more greatly developed client illustrations, given the complexity and diversity of working with spiritual and paradigm issues with high-risk adolescents. The two examples that follow demonstrate two very different cases in which this aspect of a mindfulness model can be applied, that is, the explicit intention on the clinician's part to conceptualize the client's spirituality and worldview and either explicitly or implicitly unearth such content with the client.

At the end of each case illustration is a section titled "therapist process." In this section I describe some of the subjective responses and practices I employed while working with these clients, thus highlighting aspects of therapist mindfulness that should be applied throughout all areas of therapy. These sections provide further insight into the nature of the therapeutic processes that occurred.

The Case of Alex

Alex was a 15-year-old male of ethnic minority descent and was raised in a socio-economic class below the poverty line. I first met Alex while he was incarcerated at a juvenile detention camp and began a therapeutic relationship with him in individual and group psychotherapy. Our therapy at the camp was short term, lasting approximately 3 months, after which he was released back into his community. Despite a relatively short term of therapy, I felt our relationship to be very strong. Alex often presented in therapy with issues of death, murder, and stress. He often verbalized severe distress related to his home life.

After Alex was released from the juvenile detention camp, one month passed with no contact. There was no contract set in place to continue therapy once we terminated sessions at the camp. I then received a phone call with information that Alex had been admitted to the psychiatric ward at the local hospital for 72 hours, had just been released, had been mandated by his probation officer to seek some sort of psychotherapy, and would only talk to me. We then continued our therapeutic relationship.

Upon our first meeting outside of the juvenile detention camp, I learned that Alex's admittance to the psychiatric ward had been triggered by the murder of another friend. Alex had become extremely intoxicated on illegal substances, and, in his words, his mother had "misinterpreted that I wanted to kill myself." Thus, he was driven to the hospital.

I sensitively approached his situation with the major goal of rebuilding rapport and facilitating a safe environment in which Alex could express himself. Our rapport was refurbished quickly, and Alex was again receptive to my existential–humanistic interventions. In one session, I noticed myself having the reoccurring question of whether or not Alex believed in God. I decided that this may be important in how Alex was relating to the world, and inquired about it:

Himelstein: You know, man, I've been having this thought a few times throughout our session. Do you believe in God?

Alex: Yes! I mean, yeah . . .

Himelstein: It seemed like you trailed off right there. What was that about?

Alex: I mean I do believe in God, but, [*short pause*] I don't know it's just hard to explain.

Himelstein: When you just shared that with me, how'd that feel?

Alex: It was even hard to say that.

Himelstein: That you believe in God?

Alex: Yeah, I mean, He really ain't done nothing for me lately. Everyone around me is dying!

Himelstein: You raised your voice just there. Was it because you feel angry?

Alex: Yeah. I am angry! Man!

The above interaction led me to a hypothesis that Alex's belief in God might hold important value in the meaning-making process of the horrific trauma he continually encountered. I began to develop a treatment plan in which I would sensitively ask Alex about his relation to God and then process whatever feelings arose in session. This was to help Alex clarify, or even redevelop, his worldview. A clearer or redefined worldview, I felt, might have provided Alex with the sense of a purpose or a positive framework for his negative life experiences:

Himelstein: Do you feel like there's a reason for why all these deaths have been happening around you?

Alex: What do you mean?

Himelstein: Well, do you feel like things happen for a reason?

Alex: Oh! Yeah! I mean, yeah I think it did happen for a reason. Sometimes I just think, "There gotta be some sort of reason

for all this." I mean, maybe God wants me to be strong and
able to deal with people dying. Other times I'm just like,
"I don't know why the hell all this shit is happening, and I
just want to get high."

The meaning-making process began with some ambivalence from Alex.
The next stages of therapy were to explore his ambivalence and his life circumstance's potential meanings. It was not necessary for Alex to complete
the meaning-making or worldview-building process before working on
other portions of therapy. On the contrary, all of the major phases of Alex's
treatment did, to an extent, take place concurrently.

A portion of the psychotherapy that was continually revisited throughout every stage of Alex's treatment included his resistances that arose during
session. After gaining a greater awareness of Alex's relation toward God
and the world, and what meaning he derived from his life circumstance,
we began to explore areas of his personality patterns that had been
protecting him from trauma his whole life. I would observe and name them
in the moment and then ultimately explore with him how the resistance
served or limited him. An example of the response I typically encounter
with this population, and to which Alex was no exception, is exemplified
in the following exchange:

Alex: Man, fuck this shit! I'm tired of dealing with this shit! People
always dying . . .

Himelstein: You sound really exhausted with all the death around you.

Alex: Yeah! I mean, yeah, that's just how it is. It's good though. It's
a way of life around where I'm from.

Himelstein: I hear it's a way of being where you live, and you just said it's
good, after expressing how tired you were of the murders.

Alex: I mean yeah, you know I'm tired of it, but it's all good
though.

Himelstein: Is it *really* all good? Is it okay that people are getting murdered
around you?

Alex: I mean no it's not good like that, but it's like, it's good. I don't
know how to explain it.

Himelstein: Does it make you feel better when you end your sentences
with "It's good"?

Alex: [*Pauses a moment*] I think so.

Above, I explored with Alex what I perceived at the time to be denial. He showed awareness and expressed one way in which his resistance served him. It made him feel better to employ a way of talking that would mask his painful feelings. This resistance work, alongside the meaning-making process, influenced a transpersonal psychotherapeutic process.

Therapist process

As one might imagine, working with Alex was at times difficult because of the traumatic events he was constantly experiencing. While listening to his story, I found myself oscillating between holding his story with reverence and compassion, and exploring therapeutically his resistances and worldview. I would often find myself taking deep breaths to ground myself, connecting to my bodily sensations, and feeling immense amounts of compassion for him. I strongly believe this contributed to our authentic relationship and kept me centered enough to still engage and explore his trauma and personality.

The Case of Jeremy

Jeremy is a 17-year-old, biracial male in the same juvenile detention camp described previously, and with whom I also began a therapeutic relationship in individual and group psychotherapy. Unlike Alex, Jeremy was not a hard-nosed adolescent who came from a family system struggling from below the poverty line, but rather was from a middle-class family of lawyers and doctors. He did not present with symptoms of trauma and was much more sheltered toward issues of death and dying.

Early in our work, it was clear that Jeremy and I had a strong rapport and that he was willing to engage my explorations in the present moment. As our relationship grew, so did the depth of our therapy sessions. He began to ask me if we could meditate in the beginning of sessions, and I enthusiastically agreed. After each meditation session, which usually lasted around 5 to 10 minutes, we always processed his experience:

Himelstein: What was that like for you?
Jeremy: The meditation calms me down a lot.
Himelstein: Yeah I felt relaxed meditating with you.

Jeremy: And I also felt, like, like bound to you or something like that.

Himelstein: Could you tell me more about this feeling of being bound to me?

Jeremy: Yeah, I don't know I just felt like bound, like connected or something like that when we meditate.

Himelstein: That's really interesting, because as you say that it really feels right for me, too. I feel connected to you, too, when we meditate like that. [*Pauses for a few moments*] What's that like for you when I tell you I feel connected to you, too, when we meditate?

Jeremy: It makes me feel really good.

In the transcript above, both Jeremy and I are realizing that meditation brings us closer together in the moment. It may be that the constant practice of meditation, or sitting together quietly and becoming aware of what is beneath the mind chatter, enhanced our therapeutic relationship. This may be a point of debate as of now, but it is worthy of future research.

As our relationship evolved Jeremy began to become more receptive to my present-moment interventions and personal feedback. He began to feel comfortable enough to disclose personal and sensitive information that he had never shared with another man before:

Jeremy: Man, I just thought I should tell you that I'm bisexual. I've been thinking about this a lot and it's just something about myself I feel like I can share with you now.

[*Pause of silence.*]

Himelstein: Wow. [*Pause*] I'm so honored you feel comfortable enough to share that with me.

[*Long pause of silence.*]

Himelstein: What was that like to share that with me?

Jeremy: Difficult.

Jeremy's authenticity brought our therapeutic relationship to an even deeper level. At this point in our meetings (around the twentieth session) Jeremy was talking openly about his sexuality and engaging my interventions. I was able to directly explore with him his resistances around being full out with this sexuality:

Himelstein: How is it for you to be talking about your sexuality right now?

Jeremy: I mean it's good.

Himelstein: That's great that you feel it's good to talk about it. And now that we've been openly talking about it for a few sessions, do you feel any differently about yourself?

Jeremy: Yeah I mean, sometimes I still have negative thoughts, like I should only like women. There's hella gay people though that are famous. Elton John, the singer from . . .

Himelstein: Jeremy, I noticed that right after you said that at times you have thoughts that you should only like women, you generalized the subject and starting searching for famous people that may share similar sexual feelings. Did you notice that?

Jeremy: Oh yeah.

Himelstein: Is that because on some level you're trying to convince yourself that it is okay to be bisexual?

Above, I am exploring a pattern I began to see of Jeremy continually searching for reasons why it is okay to be anything other than heterosexual. This led our therapy to a fruitful place of Jeremy beginning to become aware of instances where he was trying to "justify," in his words, his sexuality. We came to a point of agreement that there would be times when he would accept himself, and that, at other times, he would harbor feelings of self-criticism. This brought him deeper into his authentic self and acceptance of his sexuality.

Alongside working within resistances, Jeremy and I also directly discussed his spirituality. We had often discussed his spirituality and what he believed to be his life purpose before he shared his sexual orientation with me. He discussed his "spirit" as feeling more fully alive after sharing that with me:

Himelstein: How do you feel about your spirituality after sharing your sexuality with me?

Jeremy: I feel much more alive! I mean, I feel like my spirit is more jolly! It just feels right. I really accept myself and believe that God will accept me, too, as long as I keep it real.

Himelstein: I believe that, too.

The above was a moment in which Jeremy felt accepting toward himself. There would be many times to come when a discussion of spirituality would lead to the most outstanding resistances and defense mechanisms he could employ. Our primary work together evolved into a continual exploration of his sexuality, spirituality, and how they related to his authentic self. Both his feeling of self-hatred and his acceptance of his sexuality were held in session with reverence and positive regard. Resistances were observed, named, and explored in the moment to bring Jeremy further into authenticity, or what he called his "spirit."

Therapist Process

As mentioned above, I had very quickly become fond of Jeremy. I enthusiastically practiced formal meditation with him and do feel it brought us closer. When he first exposed to me the fact of his bisexual orientation, I at first experienced shock. What I did was ground myself in the present moment, by taking a few deep breaths and noticing my body being supported by the chair I was sitting in. Then I experienced a deep gratitude and told Jeremy how honored I felt. I had always wondered about the extent to which youth in this population would unveil their sensitivities in session with me. I have seen young men cry and become extremely vulnerable, but I see the majority of my strength being in an archetypal and symbolic relationship of a warrior mentor to a warrior mentee who is trying to navigate through an extremely exploited and plagued world. When Jeremy shared part of his authentic sexuality in this exchange, I was floored. I thought, "This young man really just let me hear of his most sensitive issue with himself and took a courageous risk!" This brought us closer together and no doubt contributed to the fruitful therapeutic work we did together.

CONCLUSION

The above two cases represent very different demonstrations of how the concepts of spirituality and worldview can be applied to working with high-risk adolescents. The first example, unfortunately much more common among incarcerated adolescents, portrayed an exchange with a client whose worldview was in question and who was traumatized by the continual experience of death. Much of our work involved the exploration of his worldview, the witnessing and holding of his trauma, and minimal resistance exploration. The second example described a person coming further into authenticity by way of an authentic therapy relationship and the inquiring into his defense structure. He was more able to become aware of his larger ego structure and transcend it for some moments during the psychotherapy process.

The above process exemplifies one approach to working with the serious issues of death, spirituality, and life with high-risk adolescents. The purpose of their presentation here is to serve as a starting point in opening a dialogue among mental health practitioners in the field working with high-risk and incarcerated adolescents. Further, the stance presented is a deviation from the norm in therapy approaches for this population and is, therefore, meant to contribute to a richer, more diverse set of therapeutic orientations from which mental health clinicians and interns can select in adopting their own approach with a certain population of clients.

Adolescence has been a time of growth and rites of passage for many cultures throughout the world. As mindfulness-based clinicians, it is our responsibility when working with this population to conceptualize, think about, and, if necessary, explicitly discuss spirituality and worldview in session with them in order to build upon and add to cognitive forms of therapy that are generally used with this population. This addition allows the adolescent a natural expansion into adulthood—an expansion traditionally rich with recorded spiritual experiences and teachings. A skilled guide in life, in engaging his or her authentic self, can help facilitate authentic experience, growth, healing, and even meaning-making in a population often untreated or whose treatment is labeled as a failed treatment in the absence of observable behavioral change. An authentic human encounter with an adult, another person with faults and vulnerabilities, as well as a willingness to stay in his or her own authentic experience, may be the type of experience that, at the very least, orients the youth further toward therapy and sparks a personal process invaluable and immeasurable by current research methodology. It is by this standard that the "mindfulness" in what we are generally describing as mindfulness-based intervention or mindfulness-based therapy can stretch beyond the normal operationalization to encompass the engagement of self-awareness and the spiritual path.

6

Core Themes

Concurrent with the exploration of worldview is the presentation of a number of core themes. The philosophical underpinnings of a mindfulness model of therapy I presented in Chapter 1 included the givens of human life: suffering, choicefulness, change, and human connection. It is the mindfulness-oriented clinician that conceptualizes his or her clients in regard to these givens of life (or similar philosophical foundations) and develops a treatment path accordingly. It is no surprise, given that these philosophical underpinnings of life are universal, that the core themes that have arisen in my work with my clients have at their root a struggle with one or more of these givens. I do not suggest that every single high-risk adolescent client that walks into your office or place of business is going to discuss issues that can fit into one of these core themes, or even relate to, agree with, or conceptualize living among them. I am simply suggesting that, if you work with high-risk adolescents long enough, you will indubitably hear stories and experiences that can be conceptualized within such categories. Such stories are fruitful opportunities in which to conceptualize the primary issues occurring within your client and to develop a well thought-out, mindfulness-based treatment path.

FOUR CORE THEMES

Each of the core themes I present here fall within one of the major philosophical givens of awareness I presented in Chapter 1: suffering, choice, change, and human connection. My intention is to share the core themes I have experienced time and again with my clients, connect them to the philosophical underpinnings of a mindfulness model, and give examples of how to work with such issues as they arise in the mental health relationship. These themes include (1) substance use and suffering, (2) autonomy and choicefulness, (3) human conflict and human connection, and (4) death and change.

Substance Use and Suffering

Probably the longest study investigating adolescent substance use has been the Monitoring the Future study that has been conducted by the University of Michigan since the early 1990s (Johnston, O'Malley, Bachman, & Schulenberg, 2012). The ongoing study collects data from 8th through 12th graders on illicit substance use. As of 2011, approximately 20 percent of 8th graders, 40 percent of 10th graders, and 50 percent of 12th graders acknowledged having used illicit substances at some point during their life (Johnston et al., 2012). These trends have increased substantially since the 1990s. Furthermore, high-risk and incarcerated adolescents have been well documented in the literature to exhibit an extremely high rate of substance use (Veysey, 2008). Given that I facilitate a mindfulness-based substance-abuse treatment intervention at a juvenile detention camp, all of my clients have casually used illicit substances, and approximately 75 percent meet the criteria for either substance abuse or substance dependence. Suffice it to say, substance use is a real problem among high-risk adolescents, and you will encounter it if you spend even a short time working with this population.

One of the most meaningful inquiries I have engaged in over the past number of years is the motivation underlying my clients' illicit substance use. This, in turn, has brought me to the doorstep of my conceptualization of substance use as employed to avoid suffering. I strongly believe that there are people, including the high-risk adolescent population, that engage in illicit substance use purely for experimental and fun purposes. But I also know that some people use substances to dodge negative feelings, to forget traumatic memories, and to avoid overall states of suffering. Moreover, although I work with a number of clients who use illicit substances for fun and to have a good time, unfortunately, for most of my clients, that motivation is often coupled with a motivation to avoid severe suffering.

Because substance use to avoid suffering is both important and an extremely prevalent issue for high-risk adolescents, it is the first of four core themes highlighted in this chapter: high-risk adolescents often will use illicit substances to avoid suffering. This use ranges from smoking marijuana to deal with mild dissatisfaction and boredom, to drinking immense amounts of alcohol and using narcotics to forget horrific traumatic experiences. Therefore, it is important not to write off the symptoms of a client who drinks or uses drugs just because "most high-risk adolescents" engage in such behavior. This phenomenon is a method for our clients to protect themselves against emotions and memories for which they do not have the necessary regulatory and coping outlets to handle. They are engaged in what is a misapplication of making meaning out of suffering. That is, by not engaging one's suffering on an authentic level and in the presence of caring supporters, their suffering has become (often unconsciously) meaningless and the need to cope by means of the self-protective use of an illicit substance arises.

Autonomy and Choice

Adolescence has historically been a time of rite of passage from young males and females to transition from childhood to adulthood. In our culture, it is now a time that most parents, teachers, and mental health-care providers dread. Adolescents are charged, oftentimes without evidence, with being stormy, moody, and a refuge for trouble.

However, it has been observed that high-risk adolescents, as I define that category in this book, do get into much trouble and have particularly difficult transitions from childhood to adulthood. Why is this? In historical times, when a child completed a rite of passage, he or she came out of that experience as an adult, and was, from that point, literally accepted by his or her community as an adult with adult responsibilities and treated as such. Nowadays, traditional rite of passage experiences (e.g., bar mitzvahs, quinceaneras, etc.) do not provide the same results. Our communities celebrate their traditions but do not treat the adolescent as an adult when the ceremonies are completed.

This is where the issues of autonomy and choice arise. Human adolescents have historically at this time strived for adulthood. They want to be treated like people who can make their own decisions and run their own life. They are oftentimes treated in quite the opposite fashion. Parents, teachers, police officers, probations officers, judges, and other caregivers attempt to regulate the adolescent's life to a high degree. This violates the given of choicefulness: that, at our core, we as human beings have the ability to choose and be responsible for our choices. Do not misinterpret this as the ability to choose ethnicity, class, neighborhood, or other circumstances of life into which the child is born or carried. What I suggest is that human beings are defined by being capable of choosing how to relate to their personal experiences. This is how the given of choice in human life emulates a mindfulness-based approach to conceptualizing autonomy and responsibility. By having their innate ability to make their own choices in life substantially stripped away in many areas of their lives (e.g., from strict controlling parents to literally being incarcerated and physically limited), high-risk adolescents find ways to regain their autonomy that oftentimes include acting out and engaging in high-risk behavior. This is the second core theme: high-risk adolescents who are limited in their autonomy and responsibility will naturally push back and resist a highly controlling environment.

To clarify, I do not suggest that it is wrong or autonomy-stripping to have a structured household or classroom. Indeed, I dedicated a whole section of Chapter 2 to the importance of maintaining healthy adolescent–adult boundaries. However, this is all best established under the umbrella of respect for the adolescent. It is when parents, teachers, and other caregivers and providers neglect to respect adolescents (and their inherent ability to choose and be responsible) that adolescents push back and resist the controlling context.

Human Conflict and Human Connection

The third core theme I present is probably most commonly thought of as a high priority for adolescents in therapy: relationships. Relationships during adolescence, whether high-risk, at-risk, or no-risk, can be a platform for either optimal psychological well-being or serious disaster. Adults often write off adolescent romantic relationships as "phases" or "not serious" simply because they believe they will most likely not last and that adolescents really don't know who they are and what they want. Unfortunately, this *laissez-faire* approach can be extremely detrimental, given that many adolescents commit suicide, engage in drug use, and commit acts of violence because of relationship problems. Further, it has been well documented how the effect of the peer group, especially the adolescent peer group, impacts individual behavior. High-risk adolescents are no different from other adolescents in this respect, and, for those that are extremely high-risk and involved in gangs, there is the reality of being often confronted with the literal oscillation between human connection and human conflict: to be connected to their gang is to be in conflict (physically, violently) with their rival gang.

For this reason, the given of human connection, that all human beings at times feel connected to others and at other times isolated from others, is a fruitful medium for the exploration of the underlying issues of isolation, connection, and interconnection among friends, with peer groups, and with the larger society. I can say with confidence born of experience with this population that, for approximately 90 percent of the clients I have worked with, relationship issues (i.e., romantic, family, peer relationships) were a charged topic of discussion in session that led to much growth. Because of this experience and acknowledgement from author experts on adolescent therapy (e.g., Taffel, 2005), it has been recognized that relational issues will more often arise in therapy with high-risk adolescents and should be viewed by the therapist as potential topics for deep exploration and growth.

Death and Change

The last of the core themes is an unfortunate, but consistent, occurrence in my practice with high-risk adolescents. Sadly, many of this population have an extraordinary amount of experience with the issue of death. As I exemplified with the case of Alex in the previous chapter, this population experiences premature death (e.g., by murder, suicide) at a substantially higher rate than do low-risk adolescents. As I have discussed in other articles (Himelstein, 2011a, 2011b), this often leads to the opposite of what Yalom (1980) terms *death anxiety*. Death anxiety refers to our defenses against the fact that we will one day die. The ego prevents us from dealing with this fact in many diverse ways, including avoidance, denial, and so forth. What happens with adolescents who experience multiple and traumatic death around them in their lives is a numbing to such anxiety (Himelstein, 2011b). This, in turn, influences and reiterates extremely high-risk attitudes (not being alarmed when a friend dies) and behaviors (gun carrying, extreme acts of violence). Because of this, the issue of death has a strong potential to arise in working with high-risk adolescents.

In Pali (the ancient language of India), the word *Anicca* is contemporarily translated as *impermanence*—the fact that everything in this world, everything in your life, from your emotional states to the physical cells in your body, is impermanent. This concept can be further simplified to the understanding that change happens in this universe. If you go out and ask anybody at the supermarket if life is about change, you will consistently get verification. To those of us who are existential, dharma, and other varieties of spiritual practitioner, the underlying issue relating to change is the ultimate impermanence: Our own, that we will one day die, and it is the meaning that human beings make out of their expected death that truly allows them to live fully in the present (Frankl, 1959). Because of this, it is our responsibility as clinicians to tackle such issues with our clients directly, rather than pathologize, or even acknowledge, them. Death contemplation has long been a practice of different Buddhist and other spiritual paths, and such practices alter the meaning one makes of one's own death. This is the final core theme I present here and is one of the most serious, deepest, and most potentially fruitful avenues of spiritual work and insight that a high-risk adolescent client can undertake with the help of a mindfulness-based clinician.

PREVALENCE OF CORE THEMES

As was aforementioned, when working with high-risk adolescents, you will find that some form of the above core themes will sift into your interactions with your clients. Oftentimes, it is either one or the combination of one or two of the above core themes that are prominent in any given high-risk adolescent client. Again, I reiterate that all adolescents do not deal with all of the above core themes, but that the most prevalent issues often stem from one or two of them. However, I have had rare experiences with certain clients in which all four core themes were prevalent and greatly influenced the case conceptualization and treatment planning.

Below, I present one such rare experience of a client I had the honor of sitting with for approximately 2 years (an immense amount of time with this population!) and who dealt with all of these core themes. Given the rarity of all four themes manifesting so clearly in one individual, I feel inclined to share such an experience, since it portrays the work involved with core issues derived from the underlying philosophy of a mindfulness model of therapy and a mindfulness model of life.

The Case of Martin

I first met Martin at the outpatient substance abuse clinic I work for. Martin was referred and mandated to enter treatment by his probation officer. Although Martin had been incarcerated a few times, they were very short stays and he wasn't what most would categorize as a chronic offender. He was a slender 17-year-old Caucasian–American with red hair and freckles, and was passionate about heavy metal music. He was slightly eccentric and inattentive at times, switching the topic of conversation simply because a different thought arose within him. He generally, however, presented as a happy individual. He smiled often and had no problem making eye contact with me, getting comfortable on the office couch, and talking about a vast range of subjects from heavy metal bands to football and, most often, to smoking marijuana.

Martin was referred by his probation officer because he had a serious problem with marijuana. I'm not talking about the kind of adolescent who smokes marijuana on the weekend and thinks it's cool; if anybody were ever capable of becoming dependent on marijuana (currently there is limited evidence on this), it would be Martin. He thought about it constantly, dreamed about it, and, even though he was on probation and constantly getting drug-tested, he continued to relapse every couple of months. In the meantime, he'd smoke spice: a synthetic cannabinoid that for some people mimics the high one gets when they smoke marijuana but is technically not illegal and is undetectable by simple urine tests. Martin lived with his mother and stepfather, stepsister, and two cousins in a two-bedroom house. Martin had significant difficulties with his stepfather. Upon our initial meetings, he told me he "hated him" and wished he were dead. He also disclosed that he frequently engaged in arguments with his stepfather that ultimately led to his inability to cope with his emotions, running away from home, relapsing and using marijuana, and being sent back to juvenile hall for probation violations.

Over time, Martin and I developed an extremely honest and open relationship. He never presented much traditional resistance and seemed to take a liking to me from the start of therapy. In the initial rapport-building stages of our relationship, he would oscillate between disclosing his interests about smoking marijuana and his favorite football team. He would also discuss his musical interests and what seemed to be severe familial discord between him and his stepfather. I engaged him patiently, letting him guide the conversations for the first number of sessions, playing cards with him when he didn't feel like talking, and only minimally challenging and confronting him about his role in his familial discord. After approximately 2 months, I felt we had attained an authentic relationship in which I could become more active and could confront him, if and when necessary. It was approximately at this time when Martin disclosed to me a history of a number of family deaths that he constantly thought about, dreamed about, and tried to avoid.

Death and Avoidance of Suffering

Martin disclosed to me that approximately 3 months prior (one month before therapy) his grandmother, who had raised him for a significant portion of his life, had died; that 2 years before that his cousin had been robbed and killed at gunpoint; and that 2 years before that his father had died from a drug overdose. While he was disclosing this, I found myself feeling an abundance of compassion for him and thought "so much death, so much trauma every 2 years for the last 6 years." As he processed his familial deaths, I mostly listened with compassion, told him that he was doing the right thing by talking about these issues, and offered support in any way I could. It was clear that Martin suffered from the avoidance and re-experiencing symptoms of posttraumatic stress disorder (PTSD). He talked about dreaming of his cousin being killed and his father overdosing, and of trying to forget about them during the day because it made him feel sadness, irritation, and depression.

Our next few sessions oscillated back and forth from his engaging these deep feelings of grief and sadness to his switching the subject and talking about football or music (which I noted was a resistance pattern, the protective mechanism he was using to shield himself from the trauma). It started to become clear to me that his excessive marijuana and spice use had to do with his attempting to avoid his trauma and suffering. In one session I decided it was time to explore and indirectly confront his motivation for his excessive drug use:

Martin: I got so high the other day! Man, spice is a crazy ass drug.

Himelstein: Oh yeah? [*Pause for a few moments*] You know, I've really been concerned about your spice use lately.

Martin: Really? Why?

Himelstein: Well, I don't want you to go back to juvie, and I know that it can't be detected with the basic urine tests, but we both know if your probation officer catches you he'll throw you back in jail.

Martin: Yeah, but I really don't think he will.

Himelstein: I don't mean to judge your use of it, but it also scares me sometimes because we really don't know what it does to your body. At least with weed we know how it affects our bodies.

Martin: Yeah I think about that sometimes, too, but I'm not trippin'. I think it's all good.

[*Silence for about 20 seconds.*]

Himelstein: Do you ever wonder why you use so much?

Martin: What do you mean?

Himelstein: Well, do you think there's a reason for why you're doing what you're doing? I mean, if it were meaningless, why would you do it so often and not sporadically?

Martin: Oh. I get what you're saying. No I guess I never really thought of it.

Himelstein: Do you mind if we spend some time thinking about it right now?

Martin: Yeah that's okay.

The above is a typical experience I have with many clients: they engage in alcohol and drug use and, at least on a conscious level, are not aware of or do not initially disclose their main motivation for doing so. With Martin, I had the sense that he was being honest and wasn't aware that there was the potential for him to be masking with drugs his feelings of grief, depression, and traumatic experience. However, I also felt intuitively that he knew there was something wrong with what he was doing; that he knew, on some level, that he was avoiding his own suffering. We continued the above conversation with me exploring how he felt in the rare instances when he wasn't high:

Himelstein: Thanks, I really appreciate your willingness to talk about this with me.

Martin: Yeah, I mean, I feel like I'm getting more comfortable in here, talking and stuff.

Himelstein: [*After a few moments of silence and eye contact and the slightest of nods on both our parts to continue the conversation*] When you're not high, when you're sober for a day or a couple of hours or however long you stay sober for, what type of mood are you generally in?

Martin: [*Pauses for a long while, brow tensed*] I mean, I guess I don't really like the way I feel when I'm not high.

Himelstein: As you said that, your brow scrunched. What did you think about in that moment?

Martin: [*Pauses*] I just thought about my dad.

Himelstein: Hmm. What feelings are coming up right now?

Martin: Shit. Umm. I don't know. Can we just talk about something else right now? I don't really feel like doing this.

Himelstein: Martin, this is important. Bear with me for a little while longer, and then we'll switch the topic. Okay?

Martin: [*Takes a deep breath, his brow tenses again, reluctantly says*] Okay.

Himelstein: What's coming up right now?

Martin: I just feel [*pause*] . . . I just feel like shit! I hate this feeling.

In this exchange, I challenge Martin to engage his negative feeling rather than switching the topic. I did this only because I felt our relationship was strong enough and that he would respond positively to my intervention (as in, he would engage it, not necessarily that he would like it). This is a technique that Bugental (1987) terms *requiring*, which basically refers to sternly guiding a client to explore some phenomenon of her or his experience that she or he is averse to. In Martin's case, this was for him to engage his negative feeling rather than avoid it. This is different from forcing someone to work. It can only be executed when there is an authentic relationship that could withstand a therapeutic impasse, if one were to arise.

After multiple sessions and interactions like the one above, Martin began to realize and take responsibility for the role drugs played in his avoidance of his feelings of grief and depression. He didn't stop smoking marijuana and spice, but was more aware of his choices to use rather than blindly engaging in such behavior. He began to have insight into how his father's, cousin's, and grandmother's deaths had impacted him and, after some time, was even able to talk about his emotional pain without the need to switch conversations. His ability to sit authentically with and accept his emotions dramatically increased.

Autonomy, Interpersonal Conflict, and the Peer Group

As I mentioned above, Martin initially presented with severe familial discord, particularly between him and his stepfather. I initially attempted to get his mother and stepfather to participate in family therapy, but, after it was consistently rejected, I learned that my path with Martin would be primarily through individual therapy. Martin told me of his stepfather's strict outlook on life; how he wanted to control Martin in every sense. He wouldn't let him practice his guitar at home. If he were late for his probation-set curfew his stepfather would lock the door and call his probation officer, leaving Martin with the continual feeling that his stepfather was out to get him. Moreover, given the underlying sadness Martin was feeling about his biological dad and the lack of empathy his stepfather shared about the situation, he lived in an environment ripe for angry argumentative explosions and resentment. It was clear that Martin was feeling that his stepfather was over-controlling and not respecting him as a human being. He expressed this to me in one of our sessions:

Martin: My freakin' stepdad man! I hate that guy!

Himelstein: Did something happen?

Martin: Yeah! He's always trying to tell me what I can and can't do. It's like, I just started to know him when I was 11, and he thinks he can come up in here and control me! I mean I'm 17 going on 18; I'm about to be a legal adult!

Himelstein: It also feels like he just doesn't respect you as a human being. Do you feel that way?

Martin: Hell yeah! I don't respect his ass though anyway, and I know he doesn't respect me!

Martin was extremely resentful toward his stepfather and toward his mother for not supporting him more. We would often discuss how he felt so powerless around his parents and how that would precipitate his angry outbursts and his leaving the home for sometimes days. After my hope for involving his stepfather in therapy diminished, Martin and I began talking about the choices and autonomy he did have:

Himelstein: I'm really sorry about the situation with your stepdad.

Martin: Yeah, it freakin' sucks!

Himelstein: I know that it wasn't your choice for you to end up with him as a stepdad, and that it's hard to be without your biological father.

Martin: Yeah, I hate it. It's like he's always trying to control me, tell me what to do. I'm like "I'm my own man."

Himelstein: Yes, you are. No matter how he acts toward you, you will always be your own man. There is power in that: in being able to face the circumstance you face and still being your own man.

Martin: What do you mean? I mean, I like what you said, but what do you mean?

Himelstein: Well, we both know you can't choose who your stepdad is right? And we both know that you can't control his behavior, that he's going to be that same overbearing, controlling person you've come to know. But I believe that you can always choose how you respond to him. You can choose to get angry and explode and run away, you can choose to not let him get to you (even if you really are angry). What do you think about that?

Martin: That is true.

In the exchange above, Martin begins to contemplate what it means to be autonomous in his own responses to his stepfather. This was the beginning of a long road of going back and forth with Martin about true autonomy versus perceived autonomy, his anger and resentment toward his stepfather, and his opening up to the idea that he did not have to blow up every time they got into an argument.

Although the above-mentioned core theme of autonomy and choice would also fit under the human connection theme (because his relationship with his stepfather was what was producing so much discord regarding autonomy), this wasn't the most serious aspect of Martin's human relationships that impacted our therapy. One of the more serious issues, as modeled above, is that, when Martin would get into an angry argument, explode, and leave the house for a few days (and sometimes end up in juvenile hall as a result), he would quickly connect with and socialize with friends. There were a few times in session that led me to believe that Martin didn't have many true friends, that he had many acquaintances who liked to do drugs with him but who weren't really supportive of him. This is how Martin was introduced to spice (the synthetic cannabinoid that I discussed above). He had run away from home and wanted to smoke marijuana so badly, and was about to do this, when a friend introduced him to spice.

Martin began a long relationship with spice and would often talk about it in therapy. He also would tell me that his friends would often peer-pressure him to smoke after he felt he had had enough. This was Martin's conundrum: he wanted to feel accepted, connected to his peer group, so he was willing to engage in behavior that even he thought was too risky (as do many adolescents). It was his need to be needed (a basic human need) that motivated him to take that extra couple of hits of spice after he knew he had already had too much. However, on this particular day, rather than just going to the point of getting the munchies (eating snacks) and going to sleep, he had a heart attack in front of all of his friends. They quickly called the paramedics, waited until they saw the ambulance, waved the ambulance over to them, and fled the scene. Martin lay unconscious and later learned that his heart had stopped for a significant amount of time and that the paramedics arrived just in time to revive him.

This brush with death left Martin very shocked and scared. When he told me about the incident I felt fear, along with an abundance of other mixed emotions. At this point in our relationship he was accustomed to my disclosures about caring for him. We discussed his thinking during the session:

Martin: I don't know what the hell I was thinking bro . . .
Himelstein: I'm so sorry that happened. I would have been crushed if you didn't make it.
Martin: I really appreciate that. That was too close. Man, I got to lay off that stuff.

Himelstein: Do you want to talk about what happened?

Martin: Yeah, sure. [*Pause*] I don't know what I was thinking, man. I was just kicking it with all those guys. We were hittin' the spice pretty tough and I was having a lot of fun, and then they just said I should keep going, and I know I should've stopped but I just kept going. And then I almost died! I had a heart attack and the paramedics said that if they got there a few minutes later I would have been dead for sure [*shaking his head looking down as he speaks*].

Himelstein: What's the feeling that's coming up right now? You were shaking your head as you were talking.

Martin: Man! I just feel like a dumb ass! I mean, I know I should've stopped, and they just kept telling me to do more. I know they didn't think that this was gonna happen but I also feel it's shady they ran away when the ambulance came.

Himelstein: [*Deep breath*] So close to losing your life.

Martin: And over just trying to impress some people, I can't believe I did that.

Himelstein: That is scary, risking your life to impress people.

Martin: Yeah.

At this point Martin began to realize the power of peer pressure in his peer group. He began to realize that his desire to be wanted, to fit in, to be accepted, was so strong that he would even go against his own boundaries to acquiesce. This incident happened approximately one year into our therapeutic relationship, and we went on to work with each other for approximately another year. When I first met Martin, he was an awkward, isolated, 17-year-old boy who could barely regulate his emotions and had no close friends. He was riddled with so much trauma and so many complex relational issues with a family system that gave him no support. Fortunately, when we completed our therapy relationship, Martin had moved out of his parent's house and in with his girlfriend. The last I heard from him, he was still maintaining an authentic romantic relationship with her. He had not quit using marijuana when he left, but had cut his use down comparatively, and, to my knowledge, he never again used spice after the heart attack.

CONCLUSION

In sum, when working with high-risk adolescents, it is highly likely that you will encounter some, if not all, of the core themes I presented in this chapter: substance use to avoid suffering and struggles with autonomy, death, and human relational conflict. These core themes can be used as avenues through which to explore the authentic subjective experience of your client and your relationship with your client, and as motivation for facilitating a radical shift in worldview.

The case of Martin I presented was a rare case in which all of the core themes of substance use to avoid suffering and the struggle with autonomy, death, and human conflict through the peer group were so palpable that, in any one session, we could work on or address any or all of those themes. Most high-risk adolescents I encounter have prevailing issues with one core theme, and sometimes two or three. It is important as a mindfulness-based clinician to seize these opportunities to work with these core themes and hook them into the philosophical givens of a mindfulness model of therapy. Through sound case conceptualization, we can then develop a solid treatment path and do our clients justice by compassionately and authentically witnessing the stories of their lives.

PART

SKILLS

7

Group Facilitation

I have chosen to devote an entire chapter to group facilitation in this book because most mental health professionals who work with high-risk adolescents (especially in public agencies) facilitate groups in some form, be they skills groups, substance abuse groups, anger management, and so forth. Because the process and structure of group facilitation takes priority when working with this population, I will not cover specific curricula but rather review the conditions in which an optimal group experience can occur. Therefore, the focus of this chapter will be on the process of developing and maintaining a receptive learning environment in which successful treatment may occur. A "successful group" with high-risk adolescents will look substantially different from a group composed of adults seeking group therapy. Adolescents may be more reluctant to engage in self-disclosure, and it may take longer for the group to become cohesive. Because of this, the role of the facilitator is amplified. The facilitator has the potential to influence a receptive learning environment that can, in turn, contribute to a trusting atmosphere, authenticity, self-disclosure, and overall group cohesion (i.e., a "successful group"). Once this context is provided, any manual-based curriculum or process group will be more effective with high-risk adolescents. The way in which a facilitator can influence the receptivity of the group includes (1) his or her personal qualities as a facilitator, (2) skillful logistical decisions, and (3) skillful process decisions.

THE MINDFUL THERAPIST

The successful course of a group program begins with the qualities of the group facilitator. It is you (or you and your cofacilitator) who are charged with holding the responsibility of facilitating the group. Thus, the personal qualities that you bring into the group will directly impact the outcome of the group. The qualities of the mindful therapist that I presented in Chapter 1—authenticity, intention for human connection, and stance on behavioral change—must be operational in any work with this population and in no way should be compromised in the group context. If anything, they should be made more explicit for the group. The reason for this is that, when facilitating a group of high-risk adolescents, you will indubitably face one of the most powerful forms of group resistance: the adolescent social context. What I mean by this is that, in the adolescent world, issues of peer pressure, looking cool, and behaving in certain ways in order to look cool will directly influence treatment outcome. It will be your job at times as the facilitator to deconstruct the adolescent social context in order to facilitate a growthful and therapeutic process. This is why your qualities as a human being and therapist are so imperative! If you are viewed as a part of the system that is trying to change the participants, someone else who is going to point the finger and tell them why they're bad, wrong, and need to change (and implicitly, "It's not okay to be you right now"), you will participate in developing barriers to successful group treatment.

Alternatively, if you consistently practice authenticity and human connection, and shift your paradigm on behavioral change, you will have the opportunity to align with your group participants from the start. If they view you as supportive rather than punitive, there is a much better chance of gaining respect. If they understand that your goal is to connect with them, to develop collective goals, and *not* to change who they are as individuals, they will appreciate your sensitivity to their ability to choose their own paths as responsible human beings. This is why it is imperative to continually sharpen your own self-awareness and develop the qualities of a mindful therapist.

It is also imperative to view the group context as a practice ground for you as the therapist, a venue in which to practice mindfulness. There will be many times where you will need to call upon your mindfulness skills in order to maintain presence, respond skillfully to heated situations, and/or manage your own anxiety or other negative emotions. If you view the group setting as a place wherein you can practice your own mindfulness in each moment and in which you can practice the aforementioned therapist qualities, you will model to the participants what it means to be mindful, skillful, and compassionate and will be setting the expectation for them to participate in the same manner.

FAITH IN YOUR CONTENT AND IN YOUR GROUP

Before I review the logistical and process decisions that contribute to a receptive learning environment, I believe it important to present one last issue that should be categorized under the auspices of the mindful therapist. This component of successful group facilitation is the manner in which you deliver whatever curriculum is provided. Since you are working with a group of high-risk adolescents, the way in which you present your content has a strong correlation with how the participants will respond to you. This point was made clear to me when I was working with my friend and mentor Vinny Ferraro, the training director at the MBA project, where we taught mindfulness groups together to youth incarcerated in juvenile hall. One of the first modules of MBA's curriculum we were delivering had an activity in which each youth said his or her name, and everyone else in the group would respond, in a loud and emphatic voice, "What's up!" and then enter that name. If I were to go first, for instance, I'd say "My name is Sam," and the group would emphatically respond to me, "What's up, Sam?" This activity was a way to get the blood of the group flowing and a great icebreaker.

The first time I tried out the activity, I actually was not entirely sold on it. I thought it was somewhat childish for the adolescents we were working with, but nonetheless moved forward in delivering the activity. The issue was that this was subconsciously reflected in my delivery of the activity. I opened and presented the activity with the below presentation:

> Okay. So this next activity is a way for us to break the ice. You might think it's kind of weird, or you might not be totally with it, but just give it a fair try . . . [*and then I went on to explain the activity*]

You probably noted the qualifications I was conveying in just those two sentences: *"You might think it's weird, or might not be totally with it . . ."* How would I know whether they think it is weird or might not be interested in it? It was a bias of my own, and, in that situation, it contributed to detracting from the value of the exercise. The result was not surprising: the participants engaged it half-heartedly. If I were to have complete faith in the activity, I would have delivered the instructions in a much different way. I remember Vinny's and my conversation after that group. He told me:

> When you come halfway, they'll come halfway. If you come all the way so will they. They will mirror you if you have faith in the intervention.

Of course, he was right. I tried it without qualifications in another class, and it was much more effective. The group engaged the activity whole-heartedly because I presented it with passion and had faith that they would engage it. Thus, it is important to deliver content in a manner that conveys the message that you have authentic faith in an activity, because, when you deliver it in alignment with that authenticity, the group participants will respond positively.

Alongside having faith in yourself and the content you deliver, it is imperative that you believe the youth in your group can and will engage the material you present. I have worked with countless clinicians who simply settle for mediocre groups because they do not think the participants can engage at a high level. This makes sense: if you do not believe your participants are capable, you will never put in the effort needed to engage each activity (or the participants, for that matter) with full effort. It is extremely important to have faith that your participants will "meet you if you come full way," as Vinny once told me.

SKILLFUL LOGISTICAL DECISIONS

Although qualities of the therapist are the most important factor in engaging this population in any modality, there are some logistical decisions that you as the group leader can make to contribute to receptive learning environments. Skillful logistical decisions pertain to developing the structure of a group. As a facilitator, you may or may not have the power to make all of the decisions I present below. If you work in an agency setting, you may be working with already established groups, but, whether or not that is the case, it is important to consider such issues to form a successful group. If you do not have the ability to make some of these decisions, attempt to advocate to the program directors, gatekeepers, or anyone necessary so that you may facilitate a successful group. Skillful logistical decisions include the choice for facilitation of open versus closed cohort groups and whether or not to work with a cofacilitator.

OPEN VS. CLOSED COHORT GROUPS

Whether or not you have an open or closed cohort can make a substantial difference in how your group progresses through treatment. It is essential, if you have any control over this issue, to opt for a closed group cohort format. If you continually have new group participants added, you will consistently be met with a disrupted group equilibrium. Given the power of the adolescent social context, a new participant who enters the group has the power alone to deconstruct prior group work that has occurred. This is the reality of facilitating groups with high-risk adolescents.

Consider for example, a situation in which you have eight participants in your group and two graduated before the close of the program. If you were to admit two new group participants, you would have to make sure they are in agreement with all conditions set forth by the group (which I will cover in the next section). The issue here is again dealing with the adolescent social context. When new youth enter the group who are not familiar with the culture, there is a high chance they will posture, pressure, and change the atmosphere in the group. Even group members who are engaged and participating with the current group conditions might revert back to original methods of interpersonal relating upon the entrance of new group members for any number of reasons (e.g., the new group members' status, etc.).

With the continual admittance of new members, it will be difficult to progress toward a cohesive group. Yalom (2005) suggests that groups move through a natural progression from which they first rely heavily on the therapist to "facilitate" the group toward a more cohesive trusting atmosphere in which group members need little to no prompt to engage the group. In a group with high-risk adolescents, there will always be more of a responsibility charged to the therapist to facilitate the group. However, it is also true that there is a general progression from less engaged and disclosive to more engaged and disclosive. However, when a new member who is not yet acculturated to the group enters and disrupts the equilibrium, the whole (or a majority) of the group can revert back to this initial stage. This is the risk of having an open group format, and why I suggest, if at all possible, that a facilitator opt for the closed cohort approach. Many of the therapeutic factors associated with groups for high-risk adolescents regard the trust and cohesiveness that develops within the group itself.

Nevertheless, this is not to say that, if you are facilitating an open group, you are doomed to disaster. On the contrary, you can facilitate quality open groups. You will, however, spend more time orienting new members to the group culture. When I taught mindfulness groups in juvenile hall, I taught two classes back to back in two different units. The first class was a 10-week, closed cohort group. The second class was an open group, and the reason for that related to the unit context; this particular unit had an immense amount of turnover, so that having a closed cohort just didn't make sense. Sometimes I would have a core chunk of participants who would stay for 5 or 6 weeks, and during other stretches I'd have new participants every week. There was not much progression into advanced stages of group process, but I did get very good at introducing the idea of mindfulness and group process to adolescents who had little or no experience with either of them. The bottom line is this: in an open group there is more of a chance that you will need to cover initial group agreements more regularly so that new members understand what the group expects of them. If you have control over whether the group is open or closed, know that in a closed cohort group you will have the ability to develop a relationship with each individual and with the group as a whole over time. Although this is possible in an open group, there is a greatly diminished chance of this happening.

TO COFACILITATE, OR NOT?

An important issue to consider when creating any group is whether or not to have a cofacilitator. Some facilitators love having a cofacilitator and some like to work alone. For some of you reading this book, this won't even be a choice. Your agency or organization may just not have the person power to give you a cofacilitator, or you may be an intern or clinician at an organization that believes only in cofacilitation. I have been in both positions and have many years' experience facilitating both by myself and with a cofacilitator. What I believe to be most important is that you, as a facilitator, need to determine in which situation you feel most comfortable and authentic, which will in turn contribute to the best process. In my experience, however, I have seen much more benefit to cofacilitation than to sole facilitation, the evidence for which I present below.

Sharing the Group Consciousness Load

First and foremost, the reason I believe it beneficial to have a cofacilitator is because you can share the load of the group consciousness. That is, if you have a particularly intense group in terms of life experience (and with high-risk adolescents you will see this often), simply knowing that another cofacilitator is there sharing the experience with you can be helpful. It is not just you who is experiencing the group, holding the space, but rather you and someone else, a person with whom you can process, to whom you can relate, and with whom you can share the psychic energy of the group.

Feedback Sessions

Second, I believe it is important to give and receive feedback on how we individually present in the group. What I mean is that our clinical skills, responses to difficult situations, demeanor, disclosures, energy, and so forth, all impact the effectiveness of the group, and it is beneficial to have a partner who can give you feedback on his or her perception of you. This is not possible if you do not have a cofacilitator, unless you record your groups (which a lot of adolescents probably won't like, in the first place). By having a cofacilitator, you can both depend on each other to give honest feedback when necessary. The fruits of this are that you both become more skillful group facilitators and, in turn, the group participants benefit from this improved skill. It is not that you need to give each other feedback about every session, but rather that you seek feedback when you feel called upon to do so. For example, you may have a particularly advanced topic that you present (e.g., how drugs affect dopamine levels in the brain) and feel that the presentation went fairly well. The next best thing you can do in addition to asking the participants how the presentation went would be to discuss it with your colleague. He or she will have observed your presentation and may have some specific critiques that could improve the presentation. From this peer consultation, you get honest feedback and sharpen your presentation for the next time you present it.

Processing after the Group

Third, it's important to have someone with whom you can confidentially process the experience. This is different from feedback sessions, in the sense that the purpose of a feedback session is to highlight areas for potential growth or positive qualities that should be continued. The purpose of processing is to explicitly share whatever is arising in the group or group consciousness. For example, you may learn in one group that over half of the participants have lost family members to gang violence or drugs. If the members feel comfortable enough to share their experiences and be supported by the group, they may all share such experiences. It is important to be able to process this outcome with your cofacilitator: to be able to say "That was an intense and growthful group session." This process contributes to the two facilitators' sharing of the psychic load of the group consciousness.

The other reason it is important to process together following the group sessions is because, with high-risk adolescents, it is important to examine the dynamic that develops in the group and between the participants. It might be, for example, that one participant continues to get scapegoated by a number of other participants. If this happens, there's more of a chance that you'll notice this and take action (skillfully bring it up with the group in order to use it as a learning experience) if you process this with your cofacilitator and hear his or her perspective as well.

Scanning of the Group

Following what I said above, another reason cofacilitation is so beneficial is that when one facilitator is presenting some content or leading a specific activity, the other facilitator can be watching the group members, being present to any dynamics, or helping to refocus them if they are off track. This is extremely beneficial, because it lets whoever is leading an activity be fully present to that activity while the other facilitator manages the group's behaviors.

One example of this kind of benefit occurs when my cofacilitator Stephen and I conduct our 8-week mindfulness-based substance abuse treatment intervention with our incarcerated adolescent clients. He usually likes to present the material related to substance abuse and the brain (which the youth love, by the way). He gets up and either does a PowerPoint presentation, provides handouts, or leads the group in discussion, and I sit back, listen, and keep most of my awareness on the group. I get to see the reactions of the participants as they take in the material. I make mental notes of who asked what question and who was totally checked out and not paying attention. I see who grimaces, who laughs, and so forth. It is this data that I can then process with Stephen after the group session.

Further, inevitably you will get participants in your group who are in no way interested in the material. The question that then arises is "How can we intervene in a skillful, compassionate manner in order for such participants to not detract from the experience of those who are interested in the content?" Sometimes it can be the slightest of looks, the slightest of nods or smiles that will refocus a distracted participant back on track or into attention. When Stephen is presenting his portion of the group content and participants side-talk, I often simply give them a slight nod and a smile. They understand I am implicitly communicating that side-talking is disrespectful to the presenter, and they refocus their attention, with no hard feelings. I make an explicit intention when doing so to meet participants with soft eyes so that they do not interpret my intervention as an attack, but rather as a mindful reminder.

Self-Care

Finally, one of the most important reasons I believe cofacilitation is necessary with groups of high-risk adolescents is the importance of self-care for facilitators. Groups can get intense. Sessions can be stressful and frustrating, and can elicit a whole range of emotions from you, the facilitator, because, yes, you are human, too. As I mentioned at the start of this chapter, it is important to view group work as an opportunity to practice mindfulness; to be present to your feelings of frustration, compassion, and everything in between. By having a cofacilitator, you will ensure that he or she will step in at times and help you handle a difficult situation or will simply offer her or his opinion about a topic, in order to contribute to the discussion. During these times you have the opportunity to take a mental break. I am not suggesting that you completely check out! Your group participants would perceive this, and this could be detrimental to your group. What I am suggesting is to take a "mindful breather." Let's face it. You cannot be mindful 100 percent of the time. It is important to accept this limitation. Cofacilitator intervention will give you space to take that mindful breather, and such intervention is sought basically to practice preventative self-care: to allow you to practice mindfulness in the moment so as to prevent your suffering too much stress and burnout. I wait for those times when Stephen steps in, and then I gently take a few slow, quiet deep breaths in and out. I usually do not close my eyes. I just breathe, notice the sensations or emotions I am feeling, and, ever so gently, send myself compassion. After only a few moments I can step back in with more presence than I was experiencing before or respond to a serious situation with skillful speech and action. Your group benefits from your ability to be mindful, be skillful in speech, and take skillful action. Having a cofacilitator helps support those practices.

SKILLFUL PROCESS DECISIONS

Along with logistical decisions, skillful process decisions contribute to the overall atmosphere of that group. That is, whereas the logistical decisions I described above indirectly impact group process, the process decisions I present below will directly impact the group atmosphere. Skillful process decisions include the incorporation of group agreements, methods for refocusing the group when off track, and diversity of group experience (e.g., activities, content, and group agenda).

Group Agreements

One of the most important issues to consider when creating a group with high-risk adolescents is the culture and atmosphere of the group. How you, the facilitator, envision the culture of the group is an imperative consideration and will be the proximate cause of how you establish group agreements. That is, do you envision in-depth disclosure? The ability for group members to work through conflicts? Support for each group member from other group members during times of need? All of these desired dynamics have to do with the culture of the group. As I have been discussing throughout this book, high-risk adolescents can be treatment-resistant, and, if they are not in alignment with the group, they can easily disrupt the process. Having group agreements gives participants an expectation of how they are to behave in the group. It is extremely important, because some adolescents will have never participated in a group and, thus, need to be educated about the process.

Agreements should be set up immediately during the first session with your new group members. If you start with another activity, and then a group member in some way disrespects the group, he or she has no reference as to why the behavior constitutes disrespect. In my experience, if you're facilitating a group that is anywhere from 1–2 hours in length, it usually takes the whole first group session to facilitate members' coming to the point at which they really "agree" to the agreements.

Below are the main agreements that Stephen and I use when starting a group. This list is by no means absolute, and I encourage you to critique, shift, and develop new agreements that you think are more relevant for the particular group you are facilitating. The below agreements have, in my experience, however, been the foundational agreements that contribute to a respectful and trusting environment.

Respect

We initially present to every group the issue of respect. It is our hope and goal that, at the very least, group members show respect for themselves and one another. However it is not sufficient to simply blurt out the agreements without any discussion or exploration. Consider the situation below in which a therapist "tells" the participants what the agreements are for the first time:

Therapist:	Okay, guys, the first agreement I need all of us to consent to is respect. Respect yourselves and respect other group members. Okay?
Group Member 1:	Yeah, okay.
Group Member 2:	[*Just nods in agreement.*]
Group Member 3:	Cool.

Even in a situation such as the above, in which group members technically consent to such an agreement, no real discussion of the meaning of that agreement has been explored. For example, what does respect actually mean? Could the definition of respect be different for different people? Could the definition be different between the group members and the facilitators? The answer is a definitive *yes*! This is why it is essential to process the underlying meaning of the agreement, especially with high-risk adolescents who probably have a very different idea of what respect means than you do.

Thus, you should spend sufficient time discussing this topic so that everyone is clear on what they are agreeing to. What I like to do is present the idea of respect as an agreement, and then go around the circle and have each group member (including the facilitators) tell the group what his or her personal definition of respect is. Once all the members have given a definition (even if it is only a sentence, or a couple of phrases), I get a sense of where everybody stands on the topic and can summarize for the group a group definition of respect. Then I go around and have each group member acknowledge and formally agree to be respectful in the group.

If, when discussing the definition of respect, some group members discuss definitions of respect that are inconsistent with a therapeutic atmosphere, it is important to explore the issue at a deeper level. Consider the example below:

Therapist: Okay, what I'd like for us to do now is to go around and each give our own personal definition for what respect is.

Group Member: Okay, yeah. Mine is that I respect people that are hard, and don't respect people who are soft. You gotta earn respect by smashin' [physically and verbally intimidating or assaulting] on people.

In the above situation, if you were to accept this person's definition you would be contributing to a potentially violent and aggressive atmosphere. Suffice it to say, that should not be your goal. Therefore, when issues such as the above exchange arise, it is important for you as the facilitator to remain calm and nonjudgmental (the group member has that definition for a reason) and explore the issue with the participant in depth, in the moment.

Below is an interaction I had with one group member who disclosed something very similar to the above. He was the fourth group member to disclose his personal definition, after three other members had given more socially acceptable definitions of respect. Our interaction represents one way of dealing with such a reaction and how it is imperative to pause and process this as it arises:

Group Member: Yeah, for me, respect is something you get for beating people up and not getting beat up. Plain and simple.

Himelstein: Oh yeah? Did you grow up in a situation where you had to defend yourself or beat people up?

Group Member: Yeah! I mean, that's how it is in my hood. Survival of the fittest.

Himelstein: And you've really been surviving by living in that mode then, right?

Group Member: That's right, man.

Himelstein: My question for you is, Do you think that you need to survive in that mode to be a member of this group?

Group Member: What do you mean?

Himelstein: I mean that we're all here sitting in a circle, most of us don't want to be in this group but have to, and it's at least supposed to be a place where we learn something. So do you think that you need to beat people up in here to get respect?

Group Member: I mean, it depends. This isn't the street right here so I don't feel the need to beat anybody up to get respect. But then again, it's like I don't really know people in the group, and you never know.

Himelstein: Well we do know how at least three other members view respect, and they thought of it very differently than you do.

Group Member: Yeah, I guess that's true. I guess I was really talking about being in the streets.

Himelstein: So would you be able to have a different definition of respect for the purpose of this circle? I'm not saying that your other definition hasn't served you; it really seems like it protected you in the streets. What I'm saying is that I'm hoping you can come up with a different definition for the purposes of this group.

Had I not explored this issue with this group member, there could have been severe backlash. Even if I were to just correct him and say "No, that's not going to work for this group," he probably would have felt as though I was trying to scold him or implicitly convey that his opinion doesn't matter. But, on deeper exploration, it was clear that this group member had used that definition to survive in a very hostile environment while growing up. It was one of his resistive and protective mechanisms. Because I took an exploratory approach, we were able to unpack the motivation behind that definition and get him to agree willingly to alter the definition of respect for the purpose of the group. It is noteworthy that I did not ask him to change his whole paradigm, his overall definition of respect, but just to alter it for the purpose of the group. This is one way to reduce resistance, explore underlying motives, and unpack what it means to respect someone else in the group. In the end, the group benefitted from this discussion.

Skillful Speech

Another core agreement we use is what we term *skillful speech*. This is the agreement for which we present the idea of thinking before we speak and letting other group members speak without interruption. Oftentimes, we also call this agreement "one mic," as in one microphone. When one person is talking, it's important that other members respect his or her time and let him or her finish before the other talks. This agreement falls under the umbrella of respect, as do most of the others, but it is important to review it specifically.

Safety

Depending on the specific blend of high-risk adolescents you work with, it might be important to specifically address safety and nonviolence. We continually work with gang members of different and rival gangs and, therefore, must address this issue. Below is how I address the issue when starting new groups in the juvenile detention camp:

> It is extremely important that we all agree that there is no violence in this group. The reason we're allowed to facilitate this confidential group with no staff is because they trust us. If anyone in here was to get into a fight, they would never allow us in here without a staff member again. It's important

that, if you feel that angry, if you feel like you need to fight, that you tell me immediately and one of us will take you outside for a breather. Also, if we can't feel safe in here, we will never learn anything. So I'm really asking that everyone agree that, for this hour and a half each week, we do not get into a fight in this room. Okay?

The above is also another reason why having a cofacilitator is important. If a group member ever does get that angry, one facilitator should remove her or him from the group and process with that member individually. In my experience I have only had to take a handful of participants out of the group for a mindful breather. It is sometimes difficult to do, but, in the end, is beneficial; every time I have done this, I have discovered that the participant just wanted to blow off some steam and be heard for a few moments.

The Permission to Not Share

Even though your job is to get participants to engage in the group, you cannot force this, and, to attempt to do so would be counter-intuitive and contradict the philosophy of the radical stance on behavioral change I presented in Chapter 4. That is, it is really their choice regarding how they proceed in treatment. Thus, it is important to let the group members know that, if they do not feel comfortable disclosing sensitive information, they do not have to. That does not mean that you cannot challenge a member who obviously is not sharing information because they simply do not want to. Of course, you can explore that dynamic when it arises. What I am suggesting is that there will be youth with an immense amount of trauma, and a group setting sometimes is not the best place for them to disclose such trauma. For example, I recently had a client disclose to me in an individual session that he did not disclose anything in the last group because he would have begun crying uncontrollably. In the group, we were discussing people whom we had known to overdose on drugs. He had lost two cousins to drug overdose in the last 2 years and could not discuss the situation in the group. He made a conscious decision to protect himself and did me the honor of presenting in our individual session that reason for his withholding of information.

A Final Note about Agreements

One of the most important things to consider about agreements is that they may need to be reinforced at any given time that it appears necessary during the duration of a group program. That is, do not think about them as something you simply discuss in session one, and that's it. It is probable that you will have to bring them up multiple times, especially in the first few sessions and maybe beyond that. In any moment, one of the group members could act outside the bounds of the agreed-upon conditions, and you may have to re-presence the agreements. This is why I dedicate a whole subsection to the final agreement I cover in every group: how to proceed in refocusing the group when agreements are broken or the group gets off track. Not only is this a management strategy that helps the group to refocus, but it also lends to structurally implementing mindfulness practice on a process level.

Refocusing the Group

As I have alluded to above, there will be times when, even if your group members show an extraordinary commitment to the group agreements, they will step outside the bounds of those agreements. This is only natural, and, when this occurs, it is an opportunity for the facilitator to practice his or her own personal mindfulness to whatever arises internally. In my experience, the most frequent situation in which refocusing of the group is needed is when group members engage in side-talk when someone else is sharing, start laughing about something, or, when they're feeling bored, and find a way to distract themselves.

Addressing the refocusing of the group should initially be done when discussing the group agreements, as it is one of the most essential elements of successful group cooperation. I usually present, during the first session, the process explained below as the final component of the group agreements:

> So, we all know that we're going to make mistakes sometimes right? Even though our agreement is to not talk over each other, sometimes we might, because we're only human. So what I'm going to do is, every time we get off track, or need to come back to a certain topic, if we're laughing or talking

too much or being too loud, I'm just going to say, "Hey, fellas. Can we please refocus?" Or I might say, "Hey, fellas can we please take a breath?" I'm never going to raise my voice at you. I'm always going to treat you with dignity. Is that cool? Is that a good way to go about it when we as a group get off track?

And then I go around the circle and make sure everyone acknowledges the agreement. By doing this, I help facilitate pausing, breathing, and mindfulness for whatever curriculum is presented. It is a way to implement mindfulness into your group systemically and is quite effective.

However, there is a very important catch to this technique: it can only be implemented correctly when the facilitator is practicing a keen level of self-awareness. The facilitator must be practicing as a mindful therapist, because the way in which you refocus the group, the actual pitch and tone of your voice, will contribute to how the group reacts to your intervention. As I included in the presentation above, I always tell the youth that I'm never going to raise my voice. This is the absolute truth, and I do not exaggerate this point for the sake of literature. As you can imagine, this attention to gentling the voice takes considerable mindfulness. Thus, every time a situation arises in which I may need to refocus the group, I first start with myself. I do a scan of my own body to examine any prominent sensations, then emotions, and, finally, I take a couple of deep, slow breaths. I choose my words and tone skillfully before I proceed: "Hey, fellas, can we please refocus? Hey, fellas, can we please take a deep breath right now? Hey, fellas, can we all please be quiet for a few moments?" Always, as I'm saying these words, I'm practicing mindfulness, practicing being present, saying the words in the same soft voice, for the sake of being present, not as based on whether or not the youth are responding to my intervention.

Oftentimes, it takes just one, two, or three of those requests to get the group to refocus. Other times, it might take longer. When it does take longer, most participants will refocus and breathe, and, when others do not, the members who are focusing will regulate them: "Hey, come on, let's be quiet for a little bit." And it is most often successful, because it is a group agreement everyone agreed to at the start of the program. It is a great teaching moment. After the group quiets down, refocuses, and is breathing, I often utter something such as: "It's okay to make mistakes sometimes. The nature of our minds is to wander and get off track sometimes. The group will get off track sometimes. We can refocus it just as we can refocus our minds." There have been times when a whole discussion comes about simply from refocusing in this manner. It can be an especially powerful teaching tool for facilitators wishing to facilitate mindfulness-based groups with high-risk adolescents.

I remember the first time I stumbled upon this golden technique. I was teaching a meditation class in a juvenile hall, and the group was particularly rambunctious. They had been on *lock down*, which means they were in their individual cells for 23 hours a day, most likely because of a fight. When I arrived at the unit and was told about the situation, the guard gave me the option of not facilitating the group, because he knew they would be particularly rambunctious. I, of course, did not take him up on his offer, as I wanted the youth to get out of their cells for at least my group.

When the group started, I found the guard to be absolutely right. The group members were so rambunctious that I couldn't get the group to settle down. I felt flustered at first and had thoughts such as "They're not respecting me. . . . How am 'I' going to get them to focus? . . . This isn't fun or what 'I' signed up for . . ." All of those thoughts were very ego-based. I remember closing my eyes for just a moment and letting go, releasing all of those egoic thoughts and simply breathing. Then words started to flow out of me in a very soft and stable tone: "*Can we all please be quiet? Can we all please just breathe? Can we all please be quiet? . . .*" I had made those requests about 15 times, when the group finally calmed down and we began a discussion about the need to let the mind go crazy sometimes when it's been all cooped up. If you just thought, "15 times! That's a bit excessive!" think about how long it actually took for them to calm: about 30 seconds. A 30-second intervention led to a fruitful discussion, as well as a huge insight within me about how I could handle similar situations in the future. Furthermore, as I said before, since then, the most I've ever used those calming phrases is two to three times. To this end, I have used this approach many times and heavily believe in its effectiveness. Yes, it is a good way to manage the group, but I truly believe its power lies in the teaching of pausing, breathing, and resetting when off track; a mindfulness skill any practitioner hopes to develop.

SUPPORTING BEGINNER'S MIND: DIVERSITY IN CONTENT AND MODE OF LEARNING

When I presented the concept of beginner's mind in Chapter 2 under the relational sphere of building initial rapport, I presented the attention to that phenomenon as a way in which a therapist could practice openness and curiosity, and, in turn, build rapport. Another way in which the concept of beginner's mind is applicable to working with high-risk adolescents is through group work. I believe that it is possible on a systemic level, in structuring our groups, to promote this type of beginner's mind in our clients. Moreover, fortunately, this practice is in alignment with what high-risk adolescents both want and respond well to in group: interesting and new content.

Probably the most interesting data I have collected and analyzed thus far in my grounded theory study on facilitating substance abuse groups with high-risk adolescents (Himelstein, Saul, Garcia-Romeu, & Pinedo, 2012c) is that adolescents love diverse, new, and different modes of learning. These results support my dissertation research, in which, among other methods, I interviewed group participants about their experience in the MBA project's 10-week mindfulness-based intervention. One of the themes I identified was that participants liked that the intervention as a whole, and the classes themselves, all supported new experiences in their lives (Himelstein et al., 2012a). The participants disclosed to me that they were excited to come to group each week, because they were curious about the activities that would be presented. In other words, they were not bored. This response reflects a major accomplishment for facilitating a therapeutic group with this population. Thus, there are some structural methods you may consider when planning for your group that promote new and diverse experiences (i.e., that will get your participants engaged in whatever curriculum it is you plan to present).

Beginner's Mind: Modes of Learning

First, it is essential to deliver content through diverse modes of learning. For example, a conversation about how mindfulness could help youth reduce aggressive behavior can be done with participants seated in a circle, with members at desks in a classroom style, through a PowerPoint presentation, by showing the group a video recording, in an art activity, or in many other ways. What I contend is that it is important to present diverse modes of learning to keep participants engaged. If your group presentation becomes predictable, it has the potential to become boring. Boredom is an arch nemesis for many adolescents (i.e., they often engage in high-risk behavior because of boredom).

My experience and data suggest that, with this population, it is best to have a little of everything. Some youth like sitting in a circle and sharing deep experiences. Others like watching videos, and others like doing activities in which the group is split into teams, and so forth. However, most youth appreciate the fact that there are many different types of activities and modes of learning. Thus, consider at times having your group in a circle, sometimes at desks for other activities, use audio-visual media (this generation loves that), and conduct some pure process. If you keep the mode of learning diverse, there is a better chance that the participants will feel engaged with the group—a necessary prerequisite for a receptive learning environment.

Beginner's Mind: Agenda of the Group

Alongside the actual content and activities that are diversified, it is also essential to diversify the agenda or order in which you present such activities. If you always start every group with a check-in, the group members will come to predict this and you open your group up to becoming boring and predictable. Therefore, try doing some check-ins towards the middle or end of certain groups and starting off the group with different activities. If you always do a discussion first, and then an experiential activity, try doing the activity first and then discussing it. Your group members will appreciate the different experience.

In our mindfulness-based substance abuse treatment intervention (Himelstein & Saul, in preparation), for example, at the start of the first group session, we discuss agreements and confidentiality; at the start of the second session, we do a mindful check-in (see Appendix A); and, at the start of the third session, we (the facilitators) do a two-person skit about the contrasts between reaction and response and how they are affected by the practice of mindfulness. By the fourth group, the participants consistently disclose that they are excited to see what's next. And we follow this beginner's-mind mindset with our whole curriculum and throughout each series of sessions. It is an essential method to keep participants engaged and to develop a receptive learning environment.

CONDUCT FOCUS GROUPS FOR PARTICIPANT FEEDBACK

Finally, one of the most helpful actions I have taken to improve my groups is to ask the participants themselves for their honest opinions. In the process of conducting our grounded theory study on the mindfulness, substance abuse, and group work (Himelstein et al., 2012c), I realized that the focus groups conducted to collect our qualitative data started having an impact on the curriculum itself. Stephen and I conduct two focus groups for every 8-week group we facilitate: one in the middle of the group to check in on how it is being perceived by the participants and another at the end of the group as a way to reflect on the experience (which was originally developed for the focus group to collect data for our study). What I began to notice was that, when reflecting on the group experience, most of the participants were able to review what experiences most stood out to them and why, further solidifying the experience in their memory. This is what prompted us to initially incorporate focus groups into the curriculum itself.

Since then, I have reflected upon my focus group experiences and have derived three major reasons why focus groups can be beneficial. The first is what I mentioned above. It is a time of self-reflection and contemplation for participants to discuss not only their opinions but also any insights they might have had. By doing this formally, another level of self-awareness is unearthed and the experience of the group is more ingrained in their memory. This practice is useful for that reason alone.

Second, when you conduct focus groups, you literally ask participants for feedback. In my experience, adolescents love to be asked what their opinion is and involving them in the process of improving the group for future cohorts feels positive to them. They feel that they took part in something; and they did.

Third, focus groups are good for you as a facilitator. You can get feedback on what worked and what didn't work, what activities were beneficial and which ones still need improvement or development. It is imperative as a facilitator to avoid becoming stale. You must continue to evolve, and your clients will help you in this process if you honor them by asking for feedback.

If you have never done a focus group, below are some general questions I have found useful for guiding a focus group. I recommend that you also alter your questions to the specific culture or subculture of your high-risk adolescent population, for the best results:

- What was your general experience in this group? What was good, what was bad?
- What activity did you like the best and why? What activity was the worst, and why?
- Which activities were boring?
- What's the biggest thing about your experience that stands out to you in your memory?
- Is there anything else you want to add about your experience that I didn't ask about?

If you can get your participants to consent to being recorded, I highly recommend this, because it gives you the ability to be fully present and to reflect with them on the experience of the group. You can then either return to the recording and transcribe it or simply listen to it to identify major themes and areas for improvement.

CONCLUSION

In this chapter I have presented some of the major principles in developing and maintaining a group program with high-risk adolescents. There are certain qualities that we ourselves bring to the encounter that have the potential to contribute to a receptive learning environment. There are also certain decisions that can be made to improve the cohesiveness and overall flow of the group. If you have the potential to make such decisions, I highly encourage careful consideration of the points I presented in this chapter. If you cannot make such decisions (e.g., because of institutional limitations), I encourage you to advocate for your group as you would for an individual client. Group therapy is one of the most common modalities used with high-risk adolescents because of its economical nature. It is important to have a strong understanding of facilitating groups with this population, as it can be the platform for in-depth growth for some adolescents.

8

Eliciting the Actual

An important method for guiding clients to their present-moment awareness is how we observe and respond to their present-moment experience.
As you may recall, in Chapter 1, I suggest that a mindfulness model of
therapy focuses in part on the present-moment presentation of the client.
That is, as mindfulness-based therapists, we pay attention to our clients'
body language, voice intonations, emotionality, cognitive processes, and
personality characteristics as they manifest in the moment. This gives us
the ability to track potential patterns and/or help the client engage his or
her subjective state authentically. The pragmatic philosophy underlying
this present-moment approach is the fact that life can only be *experienced*
in the present moment. That is, we can remember many things about our
past up until the moment that has just past, but can presently only
remember such experiences as memories. Further, we can think, wonder,
and imagine about the future, but can only do so abstractly. The only time
frame we can truly experience is the now.

Because experience is a continual phenomenon of the present moment,
a mindfulness model of therapy must engage the client's present-moment
experience. By that engagement throughout the therapeutic course, the
facilitator can attempt to guide the clients to become more adept at
accessing awareness of their authentic experience, which, as I mentioned
in Chapter 3, reflects Bugental's (1999) practice of eliciting the *actual*. To
expand on this point, the engaging of the actual is the practice of
unearthing the different layers of one's authentic subjective experience,
including emotions, sensations, thoughts, motivations, and resistance
patterns. If a client is more attuned to his or her subjective experience in

the present moment, he or she will have more autonomy and control regarding how to relate to that experience. For example, a client who engages his anger directly in the moment and becomes aware of the sensations that are associated with that may choose to relate to his sensations as sensations, rather than as blind rage. In that awareness, he may choose to make different decisions that have the power to drastically alter his future. This is why attunement to the client's present-moment experience is so important. It is the real-life engagement, in the moment, of what mindfulness meditation and other mental training can offer to prepare its practitioners for.

As you might assume, the eliciting of the actual (along with every other suggestion in this book) is applicable to any client population, let alone to high-risk adolescents. However, there are some very specific reasons as to why such practice is important to working with high-risk adolescents. First, research has documented that high-risk adolescents are more likely than are their nonrisk counterparts to have higher levels of the impulsivity that leads to more drug use, incarceration, and delinquency (Evans, Brown, & Killian, 2002; Vitacco, Neumann, Robertson, & Durrant, 2002). Because eliciting the actual happens in the present moment, it gives a client the opportunity to engage his or her present-moment experience in the right now and work with thoughts, feelings, and sensations that could otherwise commonly lead to impulsive behavior. For example, an adolescent client who impulsively lies is best suited to practice experiencing, observing, and regulating the underlying emotional state or experience of the lying in the present moment and with a skilled clinician. Over time, his or her ability to engage the motivation for lying, observe it, and not necessarily react to it hastily will increase, and impulsive behavior will have had a better chance of decreasing.

Second, being curious about and exploring present-moment experience lends itself to a model of therapy focused on self-awareness. As I stated in Chapter 4, this is essential in working with high-risk adolescents. It decreases resistance to therapy when an emphasis is put on developing high levels of self-awareness and autonomy rather than on changing behavior (because adolescents often interpret a therapist attempting to change their behavior to mean that the therapist is trying to change some integral part of themselves).

Third, the practice of eliciting the actual lends credence to the idea that most high-risk adolescents truly are striving for autonomy and control over their lives. That is, the adolescent life stage is charged historically with being the transition from childhood to adulthood in which more responsibility is placed upon the individual. Given that this does not occur formally, as it did in historical times, adolescents attempt to take charge of developing their own autonomy and responsibility (and, unfortunately, this at times causes high-risk behaviors). Therefore, the practice of working with present-moment experience in order to gain more autonomy and choicefulness lends itself to the increasing responsibility adolescents strive for. Sometimes, when a client inquires about my therapy focus of the present moment, I simply relay to him or her that I believe it's the practice of making him or her more responsible and in control of his or her life. Given that most adolescents strive for this, the result is often an acceptance and alignment with my interventions and a strong therapeutic alliance.

Eliciting the actual can be undertaken through many different avenues, and, as a mindfulness-based therapist I of course view this process through the lens of different mindfulness paradigms. In my experience I have found the foundations of mindfulness to be a wonderful conceptual framework within which to track the potential subjective state of my clients. The foundations are an initial tracking system that prompts me to explore certain observable behavior (e.g., inquiring about a client's foot tapping) and thus to work with my clients to unearth their authentic experience.

THE FOUNDATIONS OF MINDFULNESS

It should be no surprise that a mindfulness model of therapy references the foundational meditative practices related to the mindful path: the foundations of mindfulness. As a mindfulness practitioner who's been on many Theravadan mindfulness-based retreats, I have had a fair amount of exposure to the Buddha's teaching of the foundations of mindfulness. As a therapist who attends to the present-moment process between my clients and myself, it was only natural for me to draw comparisons between the actual practice of the foundations of mindfulness and the processes level of therapy to prompt interventions from within such a framework.

Let me briefly disclaim that I do not intend to use this chapter as a discussion or presentation on the interpretation of the Buddha's teachings. My intention is simply to present a framework for eliciting awareness of the actual within clients and how the foundations of mindfulness guide my awareness and interventions. I reference Anayalo's (2010) *Satipatthana:*

The direct path to realization, a manuscript I have read numerous times, both while at home and on silent retreats, in conceptualizing the foundations of mindfulness.

Four Foundations

Anayalo (2010) describes four foundations of mindfulness: (1) the body, (2) feelings, (3) mind, and (4) dharmas. The first foundation, the body, refers to the meditative and contemplative practices one can do while focused on different aspects of the body and is most often presented to beginning meditation practitioners through body-oriented meditations and mindfulness of the breath. The second foundation, feeling, is best interpreted from a Western society view as feeling tone rather than what we ordinarily conceptualize as feelings (e.g., sadness). Feeling tone refers to the quality of what experience is arising, be it a positive experience, a negative experience, or a neutral experience. The third foundation, mind, refers to the contents of the mind: thoughts, thought processes, and general states of experience. Emotions also fall within this category. Finally, the fourth foundation, mindfulness of the *dharmas* (a Buddhist concept that is roughly translated as "the universal way"), refers to universal characteristics that hinder meditation practice, aggregate it, and lead to insight. This is an advanced teaching that is better suited for discussion in a Buddhist text. However, because such characteristics are filtered through the ego's personality and manifest themselves differently in different people (e.g., some meditation practitioners struggle with the hindrance of sloth, others do not), in the context of therapy I interpret the dharmas as mental, physical, and spiritual processes that influence the manifestation of the ego or personality characteristics.

The aforementioned foundations have been a sound categorical tracking system that conceptualizes different aspects of my clients' present-moment experience. It is a tracking system through which my client and I can further explore his or her *actual*, thus leading to greater authentic self-awareness.

Hooking into the Actual

These four foundations have primarily influenced the awareness of my clients that I access while witnessing their stories or experience (and, of course, how I view my own experience in relation to my clients' stories). I track my client's present-moment experience by categorizing the in-the-moment presentation as falling under one of the four foundational categories. If I notice something in particular about the client's body language, I conceptualize it as body. I track the overall sense of the experience the client is having as positive, negative, or neutral (e.g., feeling tone), the cognitive or emotional experience (e.g., mindfulness of mind), and whether any resistance and protective mechanisms arise (e.g., dharmas). This gives me the ability to "hook" one or more of these aspects of the client's experience and reel it in to explore deeper its present moment manifestation, which leads to further unpacking of the client's subjective state and thus brings greater authentic self-awareness. Therefore, it is a tracking system in which a therapist can observe client presentation and, referencing that observation, inquire further into the nature of the client's subjective state. I have exemplified this practice throughout the transcripts I have cited in this book and will now highlight such examples.

The Body

The body hook refers to the body language of the client. This includes posture, facial expressions, eye contact, foot tapping, and voice intonations, among others. It is objective data you can observe in your client in the moment. By "objective," I mean it is something the client does or does not do in session. For example, if a client starts tapping his foot when discussing an anxiety-provoking situation, the objective aspect of this action is foot tapping. If you project anxiety onto that action, it is you, the therapist, who is turning that objective data into subjective (your own) data. It is only when you inquire into the client's subjective state that this can be confirmed (this can be done with sharing your interpretation, rather than asking a question, but it still relies on the client's confirmation or objection to what that interpretation is).

Let's review a small piece of transcript from the case of Martin I presented in Chapter 6 in which my awareness of some aspect of Martin's body language influenced my intervention:

Himelstein: When you're not high, when you're sober for a day or a couple of hours or however long you stay sober for, what type of mood are you generally in?

Martin: [*Pauses for a long while, brow tensed*]: I mean, I guess I don't really like the way I feel when I'm not high.

Himelstein: As you said that your brow scrunched. What did you think about in that moment?

Martin: [*Pauses*] I just thought about my dad.

Himelstein: Hmm. What feelings are coming up right now?

As Martin was talking, I noticed that his brow tensed as he answered my question. His brow tensing can be regarded as the data I observed in the moment. Depending on whether you're more interpretive or inquiry-based, you can choose what to do next with such data (either ask a question or interpret the brow tensing). I am much more inquiry-based and explorative, so that is why I asked a question. I knew that his brow tensed for a reason, probably because he was feeling some strong feeling subjectively, but I still wanted him to confirm it. His brow tensing (the data) led me to inquire about it, which then led to his talking about his dad and the present-moment emotion associated with that. This exemplifies the engagement of the actual. He courageously explored his authentic subjective state and began serious therapeutic work. This can be done with any aspect of body language presented in session. They are hooks into the actual, into the authentic subjective of the client. When we engage this aspect of the therapeutic process, we give our client's the opportunity to courageously practice being more self-aware.

Mind and Emotion

The mind and emotion hook refers to the mental and emotional experiences, processes, and manifestations of the client. For example, thoughts, thought processes, images, visions, imagination, and emotions all have the potential to be unearthed in the present moment of therapy. For high-risk adolescents, this hook is one of the most important aspects to practice with in the present moment. The reason for this is that it has the potential to hook into the other three foundations, because thoughts, emotions, and other processes lead us to the doorstep of the personality, of the body, of the overall feeling tone of the client. They are the specific, in-the-moment manifestations of the foundations that can literally be "practiced with" during session. As mentioned above, this is especially important to working with high-risk adolescents because of the high level of impulsiveness most adolescents have. Consider a situation in which a client is disclosing feelings of anger in the session. If he is disclosing feelings of anger about something or someone else (i.e., who isn't in the room or contextualized in the now), there is potential to guide the client's awareness to his present-moment experience, to explore potential manifestations of that anger, and to practice with it. This is exactly how I worked with Jose.

Jose was a 16-year-old client who was initially referred to me at the outpatient adolescent substance abuse client clinic but who ended up in more trouble and was incarcerated at the juvenile detention camp. We continued our relationship there. In one session he was particularly angry about the way the camp staff were treating him:

Jose:	Man! I'm so freakin' fed up with this place!
Himelstein:	Tell me what's on your mind
Jose:	These staff think they're all that! They take away points for no reason, or because they're in a bad mood or hate their life or something! Now I can't go on my home pass because the bitch ass dude from the dorm took my points away because my bed wasn't made the right way. And the thing is, yesterday, he looked at my bed and it was the exact same way and he said it was cool! I'm hella mad!
Himelstein:	I'm sorry that happened Jose. And I'm sorry for the inconsistency in how the staff treat you here.
Jose:	Yeah it really sucks, it makes me just want to go off on one of these punks!
Himelstein:	I'll bet. [*Pause for a few moments*] Jose, I'm interested in the anger you've expressed here. I know you're really mad and I'm wondering if we could take this opportunity to work with that anger. I don't know if it will decrease it, but I think it would be good practice of dealing with emotions.
Jose:	Yeah because I'm on the verge of doing something I could regret, you feel me?
Himelstein:	I do, and that's why I want to support you in this process, so that you don't have any regrets tomorrow.
Jose:	Cool.
Himelstein:	When you say you're mad, what is it exactly that you feel? Do you feel something physically? Do you have specific thoughts?

Jose:	Yeah I get really hot. I don't really have any thoughts, I just have tunnel vision with like an overall feeling, like "I want to fuckin' beat this dude's ass!" and my fists and chest tense up.
Himelstein:	And are you having this experience right now?
Jose:	Yeah, not the tunnel vision but the other stuff.
Himelstein:	Okay, let's pause for a few moments. Put your attention on your chest and on your fists. Take a few breaths and even close your eyes if you feel comfortable. Just notice the sensations in your chest and hands, any tightness or tenseness, or any sensation at all. Just be with them, notice how they change even if it's a little bit.

In this session, I engage Jose in his present-moment experience first by using the hook of emotion, his anger, and then by working with him to explore certain aspects of that anger, such as how it manifests physically (which ties into the hook of the body). This is a particularly powerful way of working because, as I mentioned above, it gives the opportunity to practice feeling anger, feeling how it manifests, and, over time, finding how to manage it in a healthy way.

Personality

The personality hook refers to aspects of the client that he or she uses in order to protect him or herself against anxious and negative feelings. It relates to the fourth foundation of mindfulness, mindfulness of the dharmas, in that mechanisms will arise that have the potential to either hinder authenticity or be a medium through which it can be practiced. This is the level in which we can engage our clients to become more aware of their personality characteristics, resistance patterns, protective mechanisms, and other functions that ordinarily lie outside one's immediate awareness. The goal of this aspect of the work is to identify those mechanisms that pose to be stable components of what we commonly call the "self" but that, in reality are transient, learned processes. Let's review an interaction I had with Maddox from Chapter 3:

Maddox:	Did you know Meoff?
Himelstein:	Who?
Maddox:	A former inmate here.

Himelstein: Oh, no I didn't.

Maddox: You didn't, for real, he said he knew you. His first name is Jack.

Himelstein: No I didn't know him.

Maddox: Jack . . . Meoff. Ha ha ha, I didn't get you. I get most people with that.

Himelstein: What is it that you were doing right there?

Maddox: I was trying to get you to say "Jack me off."

Himelstein: I noticed that, and I noticed you joke around a lot in our sessions.

Maddox: Yeah, you know I like to joke around.

Himelstein: Do you really feel happy all those times when joking?

Maddox: I mean, uh, sometimes.

Himelstein: Sometimes? What about right now?

Maddox: I guess I feel depressed other times; it sucks up here at camp.

This interaction (and the subsequent interactions I had with Maddox in Chapter 3) points to the idea that Maddox had a particular method for dealing with his own negative feelings of anxiety, depression, and irritability. It suggests that he uses humor to defend or resist those negative feelings. As I mentioned in Chapter 3, such mechanisms should not be pathologized, because they serve a specific purpose: they protect the ego against negative states of being and, in extreme situations, from trauma. When exploring the present moment with a client and looking for what type of resistance or mechanism is manifesting, there is the potential for the client to become aware of such mechanisms, gain insight into their origin, and learn and practice taking action with them. A person who has the ability to become aware of his or her primary protective mechanisms and resistance patterns and to choose whether or not to employ them has the ability to transcend what is commonly thought of as a part of personality. This response is associated with great insight and awareness.

Feeling Tone

This aspect of the therapeutic process applies to your sense of the overall feeling tone of the client. I have presented it last because it applies to all of the other foundations (body, mind/emotion, personality) and is a good method for generally assessing the state of your client. For example, you may encounter a client who uses therapy as a means to discuss all the negative things about his life. He may hate that his parents try to control him, vent about the unfairness of his probation officer, and discuss all the other guys at his high school whom he doesn't like. These sessions would be drastically different from someone who is incarcerated in a detention setting and instead chooses to discuss how he just "rolls with the punches" as he gets them and is just going to do his best to get his work done so he can get released. And this would in turn be drastically different from the response of someone you work with as therapist who is mandated to therapy and shows mostly indifference.

The above three examples represent overall feeling tones and senses of each client, with the first being negative, the second positive, and the third neutral. It is good to reflect on overall feeling tones of clients, because they point toward how the client relates to the world. This is not to say that someone with a negative overall feeling tone has a negative worldview (e.g., "the world is a bad place"), that someone with a positive feeling tone has a positive worldview (e.g., "the world is filled with love"), and that someone with a neutral feeling tone has a neutral worldview (e.g., "I don't care what the world is like"); however, such feeling tones point toward worldview. They are another avenue, like the body, mind, and personality, that can bring you and your client to the doorstep of the client's authentic subjective state and how he or she relates to the world.

Generally, I take a number of sessions to examine whether or not there is a dominant feeling tone underlying the client's experiences, stories, and presentation. It is a form of mindfulness-based assessment that will help guide you to a fuller, richer case conceptualization and, ultimately, to a more authentic treatment path. This is not to say that all clients have a dominant feeling tone that represents their full experience or that you can get an accurate picture of a client's feeling tone in a once-a-week therapy session. However, it does present you with data that you can then explore further. From there, you can collaboratively explore with your client the overall feeling tone and how awareness of it can be useful on the treatment path.

Sharpening the Hooks

As with any therapeutic intervention, competence in working with the foundations of mindfulness to hook into the client's authentic subjective state takes time and experience to develop. The most important aspect of this practice is sharpening your own relationship with these different aspects of yourself (therapist mindfulness). I did not emphasize in this chapter the importance of being aware of your own subjective state as it manifests through the four foundations of mindfulness while in session, but this is an integral part of developing your ability to fish out your client's experience. By practicing your own authentic self-awareness, through meditation associated with the four foundations and becoming aware of such foundations when in therapy, you will better be able to recognize such manifestations in your clients. The combination of the awareness of both your own experience and the client's experience leads to more advanced processes of the intersubjective (the present moment, authentic space you and your client share).

Eliciting the actual of the intersubjective is the application of the four foundations to the relational level of therapy. It is the unearthing of the feelings, emotions, thoughts, sensations, and interaction of resistance patterns that occurs as a result of relating with the client. It is one step beyond simply observing and interpreting data within the client through the four foundations. When eliciting the *actual* of the relationship, you take into account data from the client and data from your own experience to explore more deeply the dynamic between you and your client.

For example, I often use data from my own experience when engaging in deep listening to explore and unpack the client's experience. When working with Frank, a 14-year-old who immigrated to the United States from a South American country, I couldn't help but have a strong reaction to his horrific story. After a number of sessions and a strong base of rapport, he disclosed to me a death he witnessed as a young child:

Frank: It was crazy back there [in his native country].
Himelstein: Tell me as much as you feel comfortable.
Frank: [*Pauses, turns gaze downward and puts face in his hands*] I saw some crazy shit. People dying, death everywhere [*his brow and whole face tighten*].
Himelstein: I am so sorry you had to witness so much death at such a young age.
Frank: [*He shakes his head left to right with a grimaced face, as if he wants to say something but is having difficulty*]

Himelstein: Take your time Frank. I am here for you. You can disclose whatever you feel comfortable and you don't need to rush.

Frank: [*Takes a deep breath*] When I was eight, I was playing cards with some of my boys in the house. And you know where I live there is a lot of drug wars and gangs. A big truck rolled up and 3–4 grown men ran into the house and killed some of my older cousins, guns firing, screaming . . . [*tears flow down his face*].

Himelstein: [*When hearing his story, I subjectively feel sadness, compassion, frustration, and physically a pain in my stomach. I pause a few moments before responding*] I'm so sorry, I'm so sorry this has happened to you Frank. A number of emotions came up in me when you disclosed that experience. Right now the biggest thing I'm feeling is actual pain in my stomach. Are you feeling anything like that?

Frank: Yeah. I feel sick to my stomach. When it happened, I was sick for a lot of days; throwing up, shaking, having nightmares. And I still sometimes do.

Himelstein: And you can still feel sensations in your stomach now, as we speak about it?

Frank: Yeah.

Himelstein: Let's pause for a moment and just breathe into the sensations of our stomach. Let's keep our eyes open and just put one of our hands on our own belly and just breathe deep, breath through the sensations. Would that be okay with you?

Frank: Yeah.

Himelstein: [*As we begin to breathe deeply, I gently whisper*] I'm here with you, I'm here with you. Keep breathing, we are in a safe space together.

I chose the above transcript because it represents many aspects of hooking into the actual of what Frank was experiencing, what I was experiencing, and how we were relating to one another. The first data that he presents to me is turning his gaze downward and the grimace on his face. In other situations I might have directly explored those actions, but, given the sensitivity of the conversation I interpreted it to mean he was having difficulty expressing himself. Next, after he discloses his tragic story, I notice in myself all the mixed emotions and the physical sensation of pain in my stomach. I decided to pay more attention to the sensation in my stomach, given it was the most prevalent. I disclosed my sensation to Frank, and then inquired as to whether or not he felt anything similar. This led to him disclosing the sensations he was feeling, and to me intervening with the mindfulness and compassion-based intervention I chose to employ.

The above is just one example of using the tracking system of the four foundations to elicit the actual of the intersubjective relationship. There are many ways in which a clinician could engage the actual of the inter-subjective; however, because of the advanced level of practice and awareness needed in order to do so, I have chosen not to focus on it in this book. I hope to prepare a manuscript focusing heavily on this topic later in my career.

CONCLUSION

In this chapter I have presented a conceptual framework for tracking both objective client data (e.g., foot tapping) and the subjective interpretation of the client's experience (e.g., interpreting an overall feeling tone of negativity) to explore the authentic subjective state of the client. As therapists, we have the potential to use such data to hook into the present moment experience of our clients. By doing so, we guide them to engage their authentic experience and thus influence conditions in which more autonomy and choicefulness might occur. For high-risk adolescents, this is both needed and wanted. Further, this practice reveals the power of working on the process level of therapy, an avenue to explore the here-and-now tone of the client, of ourselves, and of the inter-subjective relationship. I contend that this is an important consideration for the mindfulness-based clinician.

9

Teaching Mindfulness to High-Risk Adolescents

In this final chapter, I present how to explicitly teach mindfulness to high-risk adolescents. I have deliberately positioned this chapter at the end of this book because of the misapplication within which many therapists teach mindfulness: as an isolated technique, while paying little to no attention to building an authentic relationship. The ability to engage high-risk adolescents in explicit mindfulness practice is strongly influenced by the conditions set forth in the therapeutic relationship. Thus, it was imperative for me to cover the building of an authentic relationship, the necessary facilitator qualities, working with resistance, and how to approach change and spiritual worldviews prior to presenting methods for teaching mindfulness explicitly. All too often, clinicians look for quick fixes and solution-focused techniques that can benefit their clients. While these clinicians' motivations may be pure, this limited use of the mindfulness practice does not do justice to the power that the therapeutic relationship and its potential for growth has when working from a continually mindful perspective.

Granted, I do believe that, if mindfulness were taught simply as a technique, it would bring benefit to the client. That is, if it were possible to simply teach your client mindfulness meditation and remove the relationship factor, there would still be potential for growth. The question I raise, however, is whether that is even possible. Even the most solution-focused therapist who denies the power of the therapy relationship cannot teach a client meditation without relating to the client in some way. The mere act of sitting with the client and teaching him or her meditation positions the clinician and client in a relationship, even be it only that the therapist is charged with teaching the client meditation, and the client is charged with learning and practicing the meditation. However, once the client asks the therapist any question in regard to the mindfulness practice, he or she activates the full relationship. How much the client likes the therapist, feels connected to the therapist, and/or perceives the therapist as someone in whom she or he can confide will impact whether and how intimately the client might question him or her. Thus, there is always context.

Therefore, I contend that the teaching, learning, and practicing of mindfulness do not occur outside of the bounds of the therapeutic relationship and that the quality of the relationship is much more important than simply teaching one's clients "techniques." This is especially important when working with high-risk adolescents, given that not all high-risk adolescents will ask for, want, or be okay with learning and practicing mindfulness. In such cases, a therapist need not dismiss his or her mindfulness orientation, but rather rely more heavily on the aspects of interpersonal mindfulness that are applicable to this population (e.g., building an authentic relationship, working with resistance, dealing with issues of change, etc.). This is why I have organized this book in such a manner.

Although I do not prioritize the explicit teaching of mindfulness over the relational aspects, there is, of course, merit in teaching mindfulness explicitly to high-risk adolescents, or I would have titled this book differently. In fact, I have had some profound experiences teaching and practicing mindfulness meditation with some of my clients. Through my experience, I have found a number of important issues to consider when explicitly teaching mindfulness that I will now review. These include introducing the idea and practice of mindfulness, the therapist's conceptualization of the goal of mindfulness, and ten concrete tips for explicitly teaching mindfulness to high-risk adolescents. I review specific guided mindfulness meditations and mindfulness-based activities in Appendix A.

INTRODUCING MINDFULNESS

The first area of importance when teaching mindfulness is introducing the topic to your clients. For that matter, it is important that you, the facilitator, have a clear idea and definition of what you conceptualize as mindfulness. High-risk adolescents may not have experience practicing mindfulness or might not be able to give you a clear definition of what it is. Thus, it is important for you to present that definition. The exercise below is one way to become clear on how you define mindfulness. This activity takes about 5 minutes, and I recommend that you partake in it prior to moving forward in this chapter. You do not need to sit in any particular posture or close your eyes if you do not feel comfortable doing so. I recommend reading through this exercise once and completing it afterward:

> Begin by taking a few deep breaths in and deep breaths out, settling into the sensation of breathing in your body. Settle into your posture as if you were beginning a meditation. Softly whisper the word "mindfulness" to yourself a few times and notice what arises in this present moment: any emotions, physical sensations, and/or other thoughts. After observing your present-moment experience, when you feel the time is right, begin to intentionally contemplate what the word mindfulness means. You may remember past or present teachers' words and definitions, the literal root of the word mindfulness, spiritual teachings regarding mindfulness, or even script from the Pali Canon. After a few moments of this contemplation, direct your intention even more specifically to contemplating what mindfulness means to you personally, not through the words of your teachers, books, etc. Contemplate mindful experiences and notice any present-moment thoughts, emotions, sensations that might arise. Finally, attempt to put your experience into words. Contemplate single words, phrases, or even sentences if you can on the definition of mindfulness. After approximately 5–10 minutes, if your eyes were closed, you can open them and, if you wish, write down whatever arose out of this contemplation, or draw a representation of it. This exercise can be completed numerous times.

After you have completed this exercise, take specific note of what arose for you. It is very important to be clear about our own definitions of how we view mindfulness before attempting to introduce it to someone else, let alone to high-risk adolescent clients. Furthermore, what arose was your understanding and your bias concerning what mindfulness is. Whether you adopted Jon Kabat-Zinn's (1994) simple definition of "paying attention, on purpose, in the present moment," or came up with a more abstract definition such as, "fully engaging present moment human experience with love and compassion," it is your bias and definition and will influence how you introduce the topic.

The most important point of this exercise is to assist yourself to understand how you view mindfulness. The reason for this is, simply because you view and understand mindfulness in a particular way does not necessarily mean your high-risk adolescent client will understand mindfulness that way, even if you have an elegant mouthful of words when you present it. As a matter of fact, there is a very high chance that your client will not understand mindfulness as you do if you do not have a very simple, short, and clear definition of it. Furthermore, even then, it may take some time. Thus, what matters more than including all the attributes that you feel should be included in a definition of mindfulness is having a short and clear definition, even if it is incomplete. The client's understanding takes precedence over having a "correct" definition.

I remember a time where a team I was associated with tried to come up with all the words that defined mindfulness for the purposes of teaching it to youth. We came up with words such as "present-moment," "nonjudgment," "acceptance," "kindness," "curiosity," "abiding," and even "compassion" and "love." With over a hundred combined years in meditation experience in the circle, this was still only the beginning. But what is the point of coming up with a whole list of adjectives if the client, the person receiving the teaching, does not understand it? I suggest here that there is little to none. I always became frustrated during my undergraduate studies when I would enroll in a large class with 300-plus students and it seemed as though the professor was just getting through his or her material. The passing scores on the final exams would be approximately 40–50 percent, all because the instructor wanted to "get through" the material. What is the point of this style of teaching? Is it not more important for students to comprehend the material and be able to apply it in life? These experiences have indubitably shaped how I view teaching mindfulness, or any material. For this reason it is very important to cater to your individual clients or groups and develop a simple "one-liner" definition of mindfulness for the purpose of introducing the concept. After you have given your client a direct experience (teaching meditation for example), you can have further conversations with your client, if you want to expand the definition. When I present the concept, I usually say something as simple as:

> Mindfulness is being aware of present moment experience; physical sensations, thoughts, and emotions.

Notice how, in the above description, I left out a key piece of most practitioners' definition of mindfulness: acceptance and/or non-judgment. I deliberately omitted this quality because it is important for the definition to be concise and simple, so that the client may remember it. Furthermore, when I have presented more elaborate definitions or conceptualizations of mindfulness, most of my clients, when asked to disclose their own definition of mindfulness, simply discuss some form of present-moment awareness in a couple of phrases.

It is important that we listen to and incorporate client feedback and data (such as I presented with group work in Chapter 7) to improve our effectiveness. It is not that I think mindfulness practice does not include acceptance, compassion, or love. On the contrary, I believe I have made this point explicitly by the organization of this book. However, what is important is that we meet our clients where they are in the process. If that means compromising our personal definition of mindfulness for the sake of client understanding, then that takes precedence. Not compromising our definition because of spiritual rigidity or ego will only leave us in a position similar to the professors I described above who are more interested in getting through material than in facilitating student comprehension. If such a situation does arise, I recommend sending yourself compassion vibrations and authentically asking yourself, "Am I invested in my client's learning mindfulness?" and, "Am I more invested in being a mindfulness teacher?" If the latter takes precedence over the former then there is ego work to be done. It is important that the definition of mindfulness, along with other aspects I cover below, be uniquely catered to the understanding of the client.

WHAT IS THE GOAL OF MINDFULNESS?

The way in which we present mindfulness is related to our personal views of the goals of mindfulness and meditation. A simple altering of the exercise I presented above, in which you switch the "definition" of mindfulness, to the "goals" of mindfulness, will give you insight into your particular ideas, biases, and thoughts on the goals of mindfulness. If, for example, you believe that the goal of mindfulness is to reduce stress, then your idea of mindfulness is very different from someone who believes the goal of mindfulness is freedom from conditions that create suffering. It is important to engage in activities similar to the above contemplation to examine where your biases and beliefs in the goal of mindfulness lie. Regardless of what your personal goal is, however, it is important to understand that the client you teach mindfulness may or may not share that goal or practice your teaching accordingly. Furthermore, they may not even follow your specific instructions, and there is no need for you to become frustrated about this. Consider the situation in which you just taught a client a 5-minute meditation, and, when processing the experience she made the following comment:

> Yeah, I really like the meditation. It made me feel really relaxed. It was like I was just really calm, and went to my special place and felt that serenity. I was imagining a beach for a little while and could feel the sensations in my body. It was really nice. I liked it a lot.

It may be that, if you are attached to the traditional definition of mindfulness, you might think in reaction to the above statement:

> Those weren't the instructions I gave. I said to be present to the present-moment body experience. Mindfulness isn't about imagining a beach or nice place. It's about being with what is in this present moment.

If the above situation were to occur, because of your preconceived schematic of how you think mindfulness should be practiced, you would have put yourself in opposition to your client's experience. It is, therefore, important to be open and curious, and to take an exploratory attitude toward whatever experience your client does have. What is important to remember here is that, whether you are a psychologist, marriage and family therapist, school counselor, social worker, or mentor, you are not your client's "meditation teacher." You are a mental health professional, and it is important to be supportive in the client's process rather than critiqueful. That does not mean you cannot facilitate meditation in a specific way or guide them toward the right instructions. However, do not expect clients to finish a meditation and tell you that they did the exercise exactly the way you conceived it in your mind. As a matter of fact, if you approach your client's experience with a more exploratory, beginner's-mind attitude, there is much potential for deepening the practice and solidifying the experience in the client's life. For example, when working with Alice, a 16-year-old referred to me at the adolescent substance abuse clinic, I found that she would often follow my meditation instructions minimally. After a 7-minute standard meditation of the breath, we processed her experience:

Himelstein: How was that meditation for you?

Alice: The meditation? Oh yeah, it was okay.

Himelstein: Could you be specific with what you mean by "okay?"

Alice: Oh yeah [*says while smiling*]. Well, I was trying to focus on the breath, but I just kept thinking about other issues. It was like really hard to focus on the breath.

In fact, I had facilitated the meditation in such a way in which I specifically said that it was normal for the mind to wander and it was okay to simply "be present" to whatever arises. But because those statements were within the auspices of a mindfulness-of-the-breath meditation in which I had in fact guided her to breathe from time to time, she interpreted the goal of the meditation to be focused on the breath. This is an important issue worth consideration. As our transcript continues below, note that I do not take the opportunity to correct her and say something along the lines of, "I actually said it was okay to be present to whatever arises." I do not address her misinterpretation at the time, because there are "other issues" on her mind. The conversation continued as below:

Himelstein: Why don't you tell me what you were thinking about?

Alice: Oh okay. You know, just stressing about this whole boyfriend thing. I really like this one guy but I don't think he likes me. He acts like he likes me when no one else is around, but when he's around his friends he tries to act all cool and stuff.

Himelstein: I could see how that would be stressful and confusing.

Alice: Yeah! It's like, "Just tell me if you like me, and stop playing games!"

Himelstein: You really raised your voice there. Did you notice that?

Alice: Yeah, I'm sorry. I guess I'm just more mad about it than I thought.

Himelstein: There's nothing to be sorry about. I appreciated the honesty underlying that statement. I'd like to pause for a few moments and explore that anger more if that's okay.

Alice: Yeah, that's fine.

In the above interaction, rather than offering her the correct instructions, we explored what it was that permeated her experience during the meditation. In fact, this led to her eliciting the actual: her feelings of anger regarding a boy she was receiving mixed messages from. The interaction ended with me guiding Alice to explore how anger manifested inside her, how it felt in that moment, and to observing her physical sensations change from moment to moment. Had I offered her the correct instructions, I might have missed out on the opportunity to engage what she was really feeling in her experience (i.e., missing an opportunity to practice authentic mindfulness). Rather, I simply noted the data she offered me (that she interpreted the meditation as needing to focus on the breath) and used it to clarify the intention of the meditation the next time we practiced it. Prior to our next meditation, I simply stated:

> Alice, I noticed in our last meditation that you said you felt as though it was hard to focus on the breath. This time, don't worry so much about focusing on the breath. Whatever types of feelings, thoughts, or sensations arise, just do your best to be present to them.

I then proceeded to guide her through the same meditation almost verbatim, with a drastically different response. This time, when processing the meditation, she did not qualify her experience at all and proceeded directly to talking about what was on her mind. Therefore, the way in which we as therapists conceptualize the goal of mindfulness, the goal of a particular meditation, how the client responds to the meditation, and our response to our client's response can have a great impact on the process of therapy. When we are clear on what our goals are, and concurrently not attached to them for the sake of our clients, we can engage in teaching mindfulness skillfully.

TEACHING MINDFULNESS

Below I present ten useful principles that have made the mindfulness meditation sessions I conduct with my clients successful. I am not suggesting that this information constitutes the sole method for teaching mindfulness to high-risk adolescents, but I do suggest that I find these methods particularly useful for a population that has little to no experience with mindfulness. Some of what I present here I have already reviewed above; however, I reiterate here for the sake of clarity and importance.

1. Clarify the Goal of the Session

For adolescents who have little or no experience practicing mindfulness or meditation it is important that they are clear on why you are teaching them mindfulness. This is a good practice, because it gives you a chance to get in alignment with your client on very specific objectives of the mindfulness practice and, thus, on treatment objectives. For example, a goal of one session might be to relax, while a goal of another session might be to be aware of how emotions manifest in the body. As I mentioned above, your overall definition and view of mindfulness will highly influence how you set goals for sessions, so it is important to incorporate the ideas and wishes of your clients so that they are a part of the goal-setting process. This has the potential to leave your client feeling included and collaborated with, rather than decided for, and influences the therapeutic alliance.

2. Non-Attachment to Formal Meditation Logistics

Depending on where you first learned mindfulness, you might have learned to assume a certain posture, close your eyes, and/or engage in other logistical activities to practice "correctly." I say "correctly" sarcastically because mindfulness is a state of mind/being that can be accessed no matter the posture. It is important that you do not stress these as necessary components to practicing mindfulness. Further, by being rigid with your clients in terms of logistics you may be contributing to the development of resistance. For example, a facilitator I used to work with would often become frustrated when the youth in the meditation group he facilitated would not close their eyes. In fact, he would become frustrated to the point in which youth noticed, and further impasses occurred (i.e., participants thinking he was too uptight). He once asked me in a meeting, "What do I do when I can't get them to close their eyes?" to which I simply responded, "Don't try to get them to close their eyes." I then discussed with him the issue of having closed eyes in a group with other participants that the youth may not trust (i.e., gang members), and how some high-risk adolescents have a difficult time closing their eyes for extended periods of time because of intense trauma.

3. Techniques

The first meditation you teach your client is important. There is a plethora of techniques that all fit under the defined umbrella of "mindfulness" from which you can choose. Some are abstract and advanced, others are concrete and simple. From my pilot grounded theory study on teaching mindfulness to incarcerated adolescents, my colleagues and I (Himelstein et al., 2012c) have found that adolescents tend to respond more positively to meditations that are tangible, such as the counting-the-breath or the body-based meditations. In this research we found that youth tended to rank the body scan and counting of the breath as a more positive experience and were more focused following the meditation than in other less concrete meditations, such as being aware of awareness itself. This is not to say that you cannot teach other techniques or experiment with your client. On the contrary, I think it extremely important to find the right form of meditation for your unique client. However, I have experienced the counting-the-breath and body-based meditations as being good "hooks" into the practice.

4. Time

Remember that, when you are introducing mindfulness to a client for the first time, if he or she is new to it, it is just as important to process the experience as it is to actually meditate. For that reason, you want to make sure that your meditations are not very long, at least initially. With initial meditations, you should be giving your client an experience as short as 2 minutes or as long as 5 minutes. Of course you will want to cater to your clients, so there may be some wiggle room. This applies only to the initial presentation. This is not to say that you cannot do longer and more advanced meditations. I once heard a conference presenter say that you should not exceed your client's age in minutes (i.e., if they are 15 you should not do a meditation longer than 15 minutes).

There really is no clear-cut, golden standard of time that will be perfect for a high-risk adolescent. What I contend is that the initial experiences should be shorter, so as not to overwhelm the client. But I have had groups where I have led 30-minute-plus meditations. This simply depends on the cohesiveness and participation of the group members and why, especially when teaching mindfulness in a group, the principles I presented in Chapter 7 on facilitating effective groups are so important. Whether or not such principles are employed and the group becomes cohesive could mean the difference between the opportunity to lead a 2-minute or a 20-minute meditation session.

5. Role of the Facilitator

If you have taught meditation to clients or to a group before, then you understand that, as a mindfulness teacher, you have one foot in the experience and one foot in the teaching. That is, you are charged with leading the meditation, so you need to think about what to actually say and have it be skillful, but you also must at some point engage your own experience so that you may observe and examine how the practice is actually affecting you. This is necessary so that, if you feel it needs to be changed, that change comes from experience. What goes alongside this is that you do not spend every moment of the meditation talking. This is for two reasons: (1) so that you can engage your own experience, even if just for a few moments; and (2) so that your client(s) will be able to engage her or his own experience without your talking, guiding, or suggesting in some way. They will get your guidance from you when you do speak. But it is also important for them to have moments where they can become acquainted with their own mind, heart, and body without listening to you teach.

6. The Use of Metaphors

There is a bit of a contradiction in what I am about to present. As I said earlier, in my experience, most youth respond well to concrete, well-grounded meditations. But this does not mean there is not a place for metaphor. Metaphors are different from abstract and advanced forms of meditations. Metaphors are other media through which our high-risk clients can understand fully what mindfulness training is about. Plainly and simply put, it is another way to reinforce different aspects of the practice and for those aspects to be taken in in a memorable way. They can be discussed with the client before and after meditations, or woven into meditations as teaching tools.

Probably the metaphor I use the most with my clients is that of weight training, since so many of the young men I work with are physically active and work out. Below is a common exchange I have had with clients when describing mindfulness practice with this metaphor:

> Mindfulness practice is like lifting weights for your mind. You know, if you do push ups, lift weights, run, etc., you'll get faster, stronger, more skilled at what you do. When we focus on the breath or the body, it's like doing push-ups with your mind. It takes time to get good at it; sometimes you'll even backtrack. But just think of this meditation practice as mental fitness.

Notice how this metaphor relates to the practice of mindfulness and not simply the definition of what being in a mindful state is. I like to use this metaphor because, contrary to what most people might think, I have no problem getting high-risk and incarcerated adolescents to meditate. Where the issues arise is in the sustained practice, and to use a weight-training metaphor has been quite helpful in getting my clients to view it as a practice and a path they might progress on. (I know some of you might have thought "but mindfulness is freedom from conditions, and having a goal or mindset to 'progress' isn't the way mindfulness is really taught by prominent Buddhist teachers." My response to such thinking is that this is not the time or the place to worry about that. Simply getting a client from this population to meditate and look inside of themselves is a great intervention. Remember, we are therapists, not meditation gurus. Thus, I caution against prescribing the client a particular meditation dogma.)

When I do use metaphor to describe mindfulness, I like using the metaphor from the curriculum of the MBA project: the lion and dog mind. When I taught such classes in the juvenile hall for the MBA project to a group ranging from 8–12 participants, I would use the metaphor as follows:

We all know what the difference is between a dog and a lion right? What happens if I had a tennis ball or a bone and I waved it in a dog's face and then threw it 15 feet away? [This is where I'd actually get feedback from the youth; just because it's a metaphor doesn't mean you can't include the participants.] That's right! The dog would go right after that bone. And sometimes that's how our minds work: we react to the first thought that creeps into our minds, the first emotion, or the first thing that happens in our environment. And what about a lion? What would happen if you waved a tennis ball or bone in his face and then threw it 15 feet away? What would happen? [Usually in a group of youth, this is the time someone would just shout out "he'd eat you!" and I usually respond with, "he probably would just stare at you, and then maybe he'd eat you."] The lion is not going to react to the bone in the same way the dog would. The lion will keep a steady ground, concentrate on you, and then decide whether or not to take action. So, when being in a mindful state, it's somewhat like having the mind of a lion; not being reactive to internal thoughts and emotions, or external events. It's about having the ability to choose a response rather than react.

This is somewhat of an advanced way to describe the actual qualities of mindfulness (and is usually best offered after the one-liner definition), but nonetheless is received well most often, in my experience, given that it gives a concrete example of the benefits of a mindful state of mind and is a flat-out cool metaphor. What I suggest is that you come up with metaphors that you feel will be received well by the specific high-risk adolescent population you work with. There is no harm in attempting to use them. If they are not well received, move on to another metaphor.

7. Process the Experience

Especially in the beginning stages of teaching a client mindfulness, it is very important to have ample time to process the experience. Being aware of whether the experience was positive, negative, or what they did or did not expect is essential to the process of progressing on the mindful path.

This is also a chance for you as the facilitator to learn what it is they are actually experiencing and to begin to formulate an initial plan in regard to a mindful-path progression. For example, it is noteworthy to recall the interaction I presented earlier in this chapter with Alice. It was in the processing of her experience that I began to collect data on what might be a suitable path to practice mindfulness with her. It turned out that it was in the actual processing of her experience where she would really engage her authentic self-awareness, and I thus catered future meditations in accord with that data (i.e., by shortening the formal meditation period and lengthening the processing of the meditation).

8. Use the Session Content as a Catalyst

When you do process the experience of the meditation, you will have an opportunity to use whatever content does arise in a number of different ways. For example, you could, if you are of the solution-focused orientation, use whatever information arises from your client as a catalyst to set short-term goals, or use it to solve problems. Alternatively, you could use the meditation experience to elicit either conscious or subconscious material as a focus of therapy (e.g., as I did with Alice above). It is my style to often use a client's comments from the meditation experience to go deeper into a topic they were thinking about during the meditation. From my perspective, this is a win–win situation: they will either be extremely focused on the meditation and not have many thoughts when meditating, or they may not. If they do, then exploring their subjective and attempting to be aware of what is occurring is a telescope into their own inner space.

9. Developing the Mindful Path

If your client honors you and they do opt to continue to learn and practice mindfulness with you as a part of treatment, it is imperative that you formulate some sort of intentional progression for mindfulness practice with your client. This is the equivalent to a loose treatment plan: you want to develop this with your client and based on your expertise, but not be too attached to it. It is in your client's best interest for you to explicitly discuss, review, and progress down the mindful path together.

For example, as I alluded to above, after working with Alice for a number of sessions, I noticed that it was more beneficial for her to process her thinking through the dyad of therapy rather than through only formal meditation. Thus, I developed a loose plan to shorten her meditation periods and lengthen the process periods. My goal was to work with her to become more aware of and comfortable relating to her subjective state. After a significant amount of time, she met this goal, as was evidenced by the quality and sensitivity of how she spoke to her subjective experience. At that point, I collaborated with her and we agreed to lengthen the formal meditation sessions, because her ability to be present with herself had increased dramatically.

My treatment formulation with Alice is simply one example of forming a plan regarding mindfulness practice, and I believe, with conviction, that the formulating of treatment plans for mindfulness progression can be as diverse and unique as the clients who enter your office.

10. Importance of Self-Disclosure

For my final point, I return to the issue of self-disclosure. As I mentioned before, the advantages of skillful self-disclosure with high-risk adolescents far outweigh the disadvantages, as long as it is mindfully and skillfully employed. Adding the additional layer of teaching mindfulness only makes skillful self-disclosure that much more important. A client who consents to progressing down the mindful path will have questions: questions about her or his own experience and questions about your personal practice. If you are not willing to answer them from direct experience, you will be doing your client a disservice. Can you imagine going to a meditation hall and meeting with the teacher, asking him or her about his or her personal experience, and finding them not willing to share it? You would never go back! Therefore, if you wish to teach meditation, it is important for you to be willing to disclose your personal experience and the expertise gained from it. This will deepen both your relationship and your client's mindfulness practice.

CONCLUSION

In concluding this chapter, I reiterate the seriousness about personal practice I presented in Chapter 1. If you plan to teach formal mindfulness meditation in any way, there is no substitute for having in place your own personal practice. It is not within the scope of this book for me to suggest a specific amount of time you should be meditating and/or practicing mindfulness throughout the day. That is your question to answer. However, I will say that, if you do not have a personal practice, an explicit intention to walk the mindfulness path yourself, you will run into issues with your especially high-risk adolescent clients. While this population might not be challenging you about the depths of the mind when they ask you questions (but do not be surprised if some do), if they get the slightest sense that you are not authentic in the practice (i.e., you don't "walk the walk") then your credibility will diminish and your rapport will suffer.

This is a different concept than needing to have similar life experiences to help your client. As a mental health professional, it would be ridiculous to suggest you would need to have the client's experience before being able to help them (i.e., surviving PTSD in order to help someone survive PTSD). The reason for this is that, as a mental health professional (at least in the model I present), your drive becomes your compassion toward your clients, your clinical skills, and your ability to be a mirror for your clients so they can develop self-awareness. The client is truly the expert, and you are charged with being a facilitator. As a meditation teacher, however, it would be unethical if you did not have a more advanced knowledge about the topic than does your client. It would be difficult for you to facilitate the work of bringing him or her down the meditative path, because it involves more of a guiding process rather than the mirrored, facilitative process of therapy. This is why I suggest that there are times, if you choose to teach your client meditation and they choose to progress on that path with you, that you will have the dual role of being a meditation teacher and a therapist. You will always be their therapist, but within the context of therapy in which you are teaching mindfulness meditation, there will be times where they look to you for explicit guidance, advice, or support. It is okay to give clients all three, as long as you maintain your awareness of when you are doing it, and do not fall into the trap of becoming solely their meditation guru and relinquishing your duties as their therapist.

Conclusion

In this book I have presented a mindfulness model of therapy as it relates to working with high-risk adolescents. I propose this model as one way, not *the* way, of incorporating mindfulness into working with this challenging but rewarding population. It is my hope that mental health professionals and authors continue to contribute to the literature on mindfulness-based approaches with high-risk adolescents, so that new and diverse approaches for incorporating mindfulness with this population may continue to develop.

As I noted throughout this book, it is my bias that the relational factors of a mindfulness approach far outweigh the isolated teaching of mindfulness as a technique. I have emphasized the building of an authentic relationship, working with resistance, and dealing with issues of change. These have been, in my experience, the most critical factors for effective clinical work with high-risk adolescents. However, the content that arises within an authentic relationship during therapy can be a medium through which growth can occur, and that is why I focused two chapters on worldview and core themes. Finally, the clinical skills I presented have been essential in my experience in facilitating groups, eliciting the authentic subjective experience of my clients, and teaching mindfulness. For that reason, I view them as critical for any therapist working from a mindfulness perspective with this population.

Although I have organized this book into three parts in such a manner that suggests that each chapter builds upon the prior chapter, it is also my hope that each chapter stands alone in its merit for working with high-risk adolescents. In conclusion, I reiterate that I strongly believe that what is needed to effectively do this work with high-risk adolescents is an authentic therapist–client relationship, a commitment on the therapist's part to practice mindfulness personally and professionally, and the conviction that high-risk adolescents are deserving of the same core conditions that Carl Rogers set forth in his client-centered psychotherapy: authenticity, empathy, and unconditional positive regard.

APPENDIX A

Mindfulness and
Meditation Exercises

In this appendix I provide nine mindfulness-based activities that I have personally witnessed to be effective activities in engaging high-risk adolescents in the practice of mindfulness. These activities can be applied to individual, group, or family settings; however, I have most often used them in group settings. I have divided the activities into formal meditations and informal mindfulness activities, which include emotional intelligence-based activities. All of these activities long pre-date the writing of this book. Thus, I do not claim credit for developing any of these activities, only for testing them with high-risk adolescents. For traditional meditations, I have left out their source because they long predate any citation I could find. Three of the activities I came upon from working with the Mind Body Awareness (MBA) project and have cited them appropriately and direct the reader to resources for further information.

FORMAL MEDITATIONS

I have ordered the below five meditations in such a way that reflects a movement from more tangible, physical-based meditations to more abstract meditations; as should be the order when working with high-risk adolescents who do not have experience with meditation (as I suggested in Chapter 9). These meditations include: (1) a deep breathing meditation, (2) the body scan, (3) counting the breath, (4) counting bell rings, and (5) mindfulness of the breath. I have written these in the first person as if I am facilitating the meditation to an adolescent or group of adolescents (with the exception of the fourth meditation). I have also inserted in brackets the term "pause" to signify periods during the meditations in which I will pause and let silence permeate the session for a number of moments. When I pause as I am facilitating meditations, I pause anywhere from 5 seconds to 30 seconds, depending on the development of the client and on the particular meditation. I recommend that you practice these meditations a number of times and figure out the most comfortable points for you to pause and for how long. The most important issue is that you are not always talking. There must be time in which the client is sitting in silence with him or herself.

DEEP BREATHING MEDITATION

Deep breathing exercises are a great way to introduce high-risk adolescents to meditation. They are particularly useful because they easily permeate a client's attention (so it is easy to focus on without being distracted), because of their effect on the parasympathetic nervous system (i.e., initiation of the relaxation response), and because of the resulting relaxation response in a relatively short period of time. My experience with deep breathing was actually the result of a misinterpretation of mindfulness practice early on in my spiritual quest. I thought I needed to "control" my breath to be extremely slow and calm when I first started meditating. I came to realize through teachers that such a practice wasn't necessary for being present. However, I did reap the benefits of such practice and still use it when introducing meditation and mindfulness-based practices to high-risk adolescents because of its effectiveness in obtaining client buy-in (i.e., they reap short-term relaxation benefits and therefore usually have a positive experience). When I use this meditation when introducing mindfulness to clients, I usually start with a 2–5-minute meditation as shown below:

> *I invite you to sit in a comfortable position. It's good to sit up as straight as possible for clarity of breathing, but don't strain yourself. Just sit as upright and comfortable as you can. I also encourage you to close your eyes. This will help you be less distracted while we meditate. However, if you don't feel comfortable closing your eyes, that's okay. Keep them open and focus on one spot on the floor a few feet in front of you. Next,*

take one of your hands and place it on your belly. Just notice what it feels like to breathe in through your belly; letting your belly fill up every time you breathe in, and letting your belly deflate every time you breathe out. This is how we're going to breathe for the rest of this meditation. You can think of it as breathing into your hand [PAUSE]. When you hear the sound of the bell, I invite you to take a few breaths in and a few breaths out, just becoming aware of your body as a whole; what it feels like to breathe in, and breathe out [PAUSE]. Take slow, deep breaths in, and slow, deep, breaths out. Simply notice what it feels like to be breathing slow and deep, notice how it feels as your stomach stretches and deflates [PAUSE]. Just keep breathing, deep and slow; filling your belly, filling your hand as you breathe in, deflating your belly as you breathe out. If your mind does happen to wander off to something other than the breath, that's okay. Just simply bring your attention back to your belly, back to your hand, breathing in, and breathing out, slowly and deeply [PAUSE]. And in closing this meditation, take a few more deep breaths in, and deep breaths out, noticing the physical sensations associated with breathing. And when you hear the sound of the meditation bell, listen to the tone until you can't hear it any longer; feeling and hearing the vibrations. When you can't hear the bell or feel the vibrations any longer, gently open your eyes and expand your awareness from the inner world to encompass the outer world too.

This meditation need not be long. As a matter of fact, it is a good idea to keep it to 5 minutes and under simply because it can make some clients feel light-headed. And remember, do not worry that this is not a traditional mindfulness practice. As I suggested in Chapter 9, the goal with mindfulness practice is to give clients an opportunity to explore it, rather than have them practice mindfulness from a particular dogma. If this practice sparks an interest in meditation or mindfulness, it means it was successful. If it does not, keep exploring other meditations and mindfulness activities.

THE BODY SCAN MEDITATION

The body scan meditation is a widely used mindfulness meditation. I first learned it on an S. N. Goenka Vipassana retreat many years ago. That experience has influenced teaching the body scan with high-risk adolescents; however, this meditation does not reflect Goenka's traditional teaching. As with all meditations, it is important to start by guiding your client to a comfortable posture:

> *I invite you to sit in a comfortable position. It's good to sit up as straight as possible for clarity of breathing, but don't strain yourself. Just sit as upright and comfortable as you can. I also encourage you to close your eyes. This will help you be less distracted while we meditate. However, if you don't feel comfortable closing your eyes, that's okay. Keep them open and focus on one spot on the floor a few feet in front of you. When you hear the sound of the bell, I invite you to take a few breaths in and a few breaths out, just becoming aware of your body as a whole [PAUSE]. Begin by shifting all of your attention to your feet. You might notice any sensation you can feel in your feet. Maybe just the feel of your shoes on the floor, or a specific sensation such as heat or moisture. Just observe whatever is there [PAUSE]. Next, move your awareness to your ankle and lower legs, noticing any sensation. You might feel a tingling sensation, or heat, or other sensations. Or maybe you feel your pant leg, or how it feels against your leg. Anything you feel is okay, even if you can't feel anything at all. Just keep your awareness on that area of the body for the next few moments [PAUSE]. Next, move your awareness into your knees, noticing the front, back, and sides of your knees [PAUSE]. Next, move your awareness up into the top of your legs; the quadriceps, hamstrings, inner and outer thighs. You might feel the support of the chair or cushion under you, your muscles, tingling, or any sensation [PAUSE]. If your mind wanders, that's okay; gently bring it back to the area of the body you were focusing on, no need to get frustrated if it wanders a lot. Whatever your mind goes to, be present to that, and then return to the area of the body we're focusing on. Next, shift your awareness into your belly. Notice what if feels like to breath in and breath out. Notice how the muscles in your stomach stretch*

when it fills with air; notice all the sensations that come along with breathing in and breathing out. Now shift your awareness up into your chest, noticing the physical sensations associated with breathing in and out of your chest [PAUSE]. Next, shift your awareness down into your lower back. Let your awareness slowly rise up your back as if a cup is filling up with water [PAUSE]. You might feel tension from sitting up straight, or you might feel the back of the chair supporting you. Just notice all the little sensations that make up those feelings in your back. And again, if your mind wanders, that's okay. Gently bring it back to the area of the body we're focusing on. No need to get frustrated if it wanders often, whatever your mind goes to, be present to that, and then return to the area of the body we're focusing on. Then shift all of your awareness to your hands. Start out by feeling your fingertips, noticing any sensations there. Slowly let your awareness move into your fingers, knuckles, and to the base of your hands [PAUSE]. Let your awareness crawl through your wrists, and up into your forearms and elbows. You might notice any sensation. Let your awareness move into your upper arms; biceps, triceps, and shoulders. Next let your awareness move to the base of your neck, and up into the next; the front, back, and sides of the neck [PAUSE]. Let your awareness rise into your chin, into your jaw and mouth. Become aware of all the little sensations when focusing on your jaw and mouth. Maybe your jaw is clenched. Maybe it's loose. It doesn't matter how it is, just be aware of it. Move your awareness up into your nose, eyebrow, and eye areas [PAUSE]. And cheeks and ears. Let your awareness shift to your forehead, and notice your face as a whole; any sensations, any itches, any tingling [PAUSE]. Shift your awareness to the back and sides of your head. And finally to the very top of your head [PAUSE]. Now see if you can shift your awareness to your whole body; from the top of your head to the tips of your toes. See if you can notice any sensation, whether it be your breath as it comes in and out, a specific sensation, or anything else that arises [PAUSE]. As you keep your awareness on the body and sensations, see how they might change, even very subtly, from moment to moment. Notice this change in different parts of the body [PAUSE]. And in closing this meditation, take a few more deep breaths in, and deep breaths out, noticing the physical sensations associated with breathing. And when you hear the sound of the meditation bell, listen to the tone until you can't hear it any longer; feeling and hearing the vibrations. When you can't hear the bell or feel the vibrations any longer, gently open your eyes and expand your awareness from the inner world to encompass the outer world too.

In the above body scan meditation I guide the client through the specific parts of the physical body. As they progress through the body scan practice, you can omit more formal instructions and gently guide them through bulk parts of the body (e.g., legs). You might also become subtler in your teaching, spending longer periods on each body part. In time, your client will be able to practice the body scan without your instruction. This is a great, introductory 5-minute meditation. However, it can easily be extended by making the instruction subtler or repeating the body scan. I most often use this meditation in the early stages with adolescents, but have done 30-minute body scans in the past.

COUNTING THE BREATH

Counting the breath is another great way to get high-risk adolescents involved in mental focusing. In the pilot grounded theory study my colleagues and I conducted (Himelstein et al., 2012c), most participants disclosed that the counting the breath meditation left them feeling most focused out of all the meditations they practiced. It is a good way to introduce a mindfulness of the breath (the meditation I present at the end of this section) because it orients the client to the breath and gives them a non-abstract object to focus on (the number). I first learned counting of the breath when I started meditating in high school, through Zazen Zen meditation. Again, I quickly learned that counting wasn't necessary to practice Zazen, but given its impact on me during my early stages of learning meditation it always stuck as a formidable experience. I also recommend this meditation to be shorter (3–5 minutes). When working with high-risk adolescents, I present it as I do here:

I invite you to sit in a comfortable position. It's good to sit up as straight as possible for clarity of breathing, but don't strain yourself. Just sit as upright and comfortable as you can. I also encourage you to close your eyes. This will help you be less distracted while we meditate. However, if you don't feel comfortable closing your eyes, that's okay. Keep them open and focus on one spot on the floor a few feet in front of you. I'm going to teach you how to count your breaths. For your first breath in, count one. For your first breath out count two. And go all the way up until you reach 10. Once you reach 10, start over at one. You can simply just say "one" or whatever the number is to yourself silently, you can think of the image of the number, or your can extend the saying of the number for the whole breath like, "Oooooonnnnneeeeeee." Do whatever feels most comfortable, just stay consistent throughout the whole meditation [PAUSE]. When you hear the sound of the bell, I invite you to begin by counting your first breath in, and your first breath out [PAUSE]. Count each breath in, and count each breath out. When you reach 10, start over again at one [PAUSE]. Just keep breathing and focusing on the number that you are currently on. If your mind does happen to wander off to something other than the breath or the number, that's okay. Just simply bring your attention back to your breath, back to the last number you can remember, and start again [PAUSE]. Breathing in, and breathing out. Simply focus on the number breath you are counting. Once you reach 10, start again at one [PAUSE]. And in closing this meditation, finish counting your breaths until you reach 10 [PAUSE]. And when you hear the sound of the meditation bell, listen to the tone until you can't hear it any longer; feeling and hearing the vibrations. When you can't hear the bell or feel the vibrations any longer, gently open your eyes and expand your awareness from the inner world to encompass the outer world too.

Counting the breath is great as a training tool for the traditional mindfulness of the breath meditation. It gives the novice a very specific object to focus on that can be gradually removed. For example, after working with your client for some time, you might have him or her only count in-breaths, or only count out-breaths. In time, you may have her or him count no breaths and simply be present to the breath.

COUNTING RINGS

The counting rings meditation is something I learned in my work with the MBA project. The MBA project uses it in their curriculum in a module dedicated to introducing mindfulness. It is a formal, but wonderful method in getting high-risk adolescents acquainted with how their minds work on an introductory level. Because the nature of this meditation lies within the implementation of ringing meditation bells, I present it here in the third person:

> *Invite your client or group to sit in a comfortable position and close their eyes or keep them open, as with the other meditations. Once they have assumed this position and are ready to begin, notify your client or group that you will be ringing the meditation bell a number of times throughout the meditation. Tell the client or group to keep a count of how many times the meditation bell is being rung. Also tell the client or group they may only use their mind to keep count. That is, they cannot use their hands and fingers to keep count. Once they acknowledge these agreements, alert the client or group that you are about to ring the bell for the first time. Prior to ringing the bell, choose a number of times to ring the bell and stay true to that number. Ring the bell for the first time and pause. Then go on to ring the bell the total number of times you have chosen with different lengths of time in between each ring. That is, you might wait 30 seconds after the first ring, 10 seconds after the second ring, 60 seconds after the third ring, and so on. This is so your client or group will not become accustomed to a particular time period elapsing in between rings. Before your final ring, notify your client or group that this will be the last ring, and direct them to listen to the bell until they cannot hear it any longer. Once the sound of the bell has stopped, have your client or the group members open their eyes (if they were closed) and ask them how many times they thought the bell had been rung. Before disclosing the answer, ask your client or group members how they remembered which number ring they were on. Did they repeat the number continuously until the next bell rang? Did they simply say the number once and wait until the next bell? Did they see an image? If you are working with a group, go around the circle or*

group and ask as many participants that are willing to share. After this process you can disclose the actual number of times you rang the bell.

This is a good meditation exercise because it lends to the discussion of how the mind works during the "in-between" states. Between the first ring and the next, each client's mind may do something somewhat different. It is beneficial to discuss this because not only does the client increase an awareness of how the mind tends to focus or not focus, but you as the therapist/facilitator also get a sneak peek into the mind of each of your clients.

MINDFULNESS OF THE BREATH

Mindfulness of the breath is probably the most taught meditation that is associated with the practice of mindfulness. I have placed it at the end of this formal meditation section because in my experience some adolescents have alluded to the idea that it is abstract and difficult. However, some adolescents really like this meditation and I believe that whether or not your client is fond of it or finds it easy or difficult, it is useful. Use your clinical discernment when teaching this meditation; as I said in Chapter 9 and above, I usually present other meditations before this one. When I facilitate this meditation I keep three general statements in mind to remind the client(s) during the meditation: (1) if the mind wanders, gently bring it back to the breath; (2) it is okay that the mind wanders; (3) there's no need to get frustrated if the mind is not doing what you want it to, the practice is to just be present to whatever is in your present moment experience. I make sure to interweave those statements into the mindfulness of the breath practice at the very least once, but usually more, depending on the length of the meditation. It is important to begin the meditation with an invitation, as in the above meditations. However, because in this meditation there will be more silence and time without you talking, I have found it useful to be mindful of my tone, guidance, and specific words I choose. I usually facilitate mindfulness of the breath as presented below:

I invite you to sit in a comfortable position. It's good to sit up as straight as possible for clarity of breathing, but don't strain yourself. Just sit as upright and comfortable as you can. I also encourage you to close your eyes. This will help you be less distracted while we meditate. However, if you don't feel comfortable closing your eyes, that's okay. Keep them open and focus on one spot on the floor a few feet in front of you. When you hear the sound of the bell, I invite you to take a few breaths in and a few breaths out, just becoming aware of your body as a whole [PAUSE]. I encourage you to begin by becoming aware of your breath. Become aware of your breath as you inhale, and as you exhale [PAUSE]. Notice in your body the place where you feel your breath the most; it could be your nostrils, it could be your stomach or chest, or even your mouth if that's where you're breathing from. Wherever you find it easiest to focus, let your attention settle there [PAUSE]. You may notice that you're breathing deep. You may notice that you're breathing shallow. It really doesn't matter if you're breathing deep or shallow. If you're breathing deep, just notice that you're breathing deep. If you're breathing shallow, just notice that you're breathing shallow [PAUSE]. Breathing in and breathing out. Breathing in and breathing out, if you notice that your mind wanders off the breath, maybe thinking about the future, or the past, that's okay. Gently bring your awareness back to the present moment by becoming aware of your breathing. If your mind goes to thoughts, feelings, or sensations, that's okay. There's no need to get frustrated if your mind continues to wander, just be present to whatever your mind goes to, and then gently bring your awareness back to your breath. If you find it hard to focus, take a couple deep breaths in and deep breaths out and then return to normal breathing [PAUSE]. Breathing in and breathing out, notice your breath right here, right now in the present moment. Notice the physical sensations associated with breathing. Witness your body living in this moment [PAUSE]. And in closing this meditation, take a few more deep breaths in, and deep breaths out, noticing the physical sensations associated with breathing. And when you hear the sound of the meditation bell, listen to the tone until you can't hear it any longer. When you can't hear the bell, gently open your eyes and expand your awareness from the inner world to encompass the outer world too.

The above steps can be repeated as many times as necessary. The above transcript is from an approximately 5-minute meditation. If you wish to extend the meditation, simply repeat the steps as necessary. Remember, for this meditation it is imperative that you are not always talking; you want to let your client experience what it is like to get acquainted with her or his subjective experience. This is why it can be hard for clients to focus during this meditation in the beginning stages if they have not developed any concentration.

When using this with a single client, I like to get in tune with his or her breathing rhythm. As s/he breathes in, I make the statement about breathing in, as s/he breaths out, I make the statement about breathing out. Clients often report they feel very in tune and have a strong meditation experience when I present those instructions in unisom with their breathing process.

MINDFULNESS-BASED ACTIVITIES

Below are four informal mindfulness-based activities I have used with high-risk adolescents. All activities are best suited for group work but can be implemented in individual and sometimes family settings. These activities include: (1) the mindful check-in, (2) mindful eating, (3) "Still Chillen", and (4) "Stand If."

Mindful Check-In

I stumbled upon the mindful check-in while facilitating the mindfulness-based substance abuse group with my cofacilitator Stephen. A participant was feeling particularly frustrated one day while in the group and before he checked in took a few deep breaths and spoke his truth. From then on out, Stephen and I formally implemented it into our curriculum as a way to teach mindfulness informally without meditating. This activity can be used in group, individual, or family psychotherapy in lieu of a regular check-in in which the therapist may ask a client to speak about how s/he feels using either their own subjective rating or an objective scale rating (e.g., "on a 1–10, how are you today?"). The difference between a regular check-in and a mindful check-in is that you always ask the client to check in about his or her experience in the present moment. Staying specific to the present moment will allow the client to become more familiar with accessing his or her present moment experience and thus become more skilled in mindfulness. A mindful check-in consists of taking one or two deep breaths prior to disclosing one's present-moment experience. Use the following four steps as a guide to implementing the mindful check-in before putting your own twist on the exercise:

1. Remind the group what you mean when you say "check-in" and encourage them to keep their awareness on the present moment when thinking about their experience:

     Facilitator: Remember that in a check-in, you can speak about your thoughts (what you're thinking about), your feelings (the emotions you are having), or your physical state of being (sensations). When you think about any of those, do your best to keep your awareness on what's going on with you in the here and now, in the present moment.

2. Before starting, instruct each group participant to take a deep breath before thinking about their experience and checking-in:

     Facilitator: Before you check-in, what I want to encourage you to do is take a deep breath in, and a deep breath out fully, and then check in on any part of your experience in the present moment. After everyone is done, we'll talk about the significance of taking the breath and why it's important for the check-in.

3. Ask for a volunteer to go first, make sure s/he takes the deep breath and talks about the present moment, and then go in a circle until everyone is done.

4. Process why the deep breath is important. First ask the group why they thought it was important, and then guide the discussion to at least the following points: (a) taking a breath gives you another moment to really check-in and become aware of your experience, (b) taking a breath gives you a chance to calm down mentally and emotionally, and (c), taking a breath calms the body down physiologically and activates stress relieving endorphins.

What's wonderful about this activity is that if you implement it early in your group (Stephen and I implement it on the first session) and keep it as a practice, group members will begin to use the mindful check-in whenever you ask them to check in and not need to be reminded to take a deep breath. Usually by about the fourth or fifth group session in our program participants do not need to be reminded to take a deep breath or speak first about their present-moment experience. By this point in the program participants are taking time, pausing, and really checking in with how they feel. To that end, I feel very strongly about this activity as an enhancer of mindfulness.

Mindful Eating Exercises

Mindful eating exercises have long been a practice of many traditions, and this exercise was probably made most famous in Western society by John Kabat-Zinn's raisin exercise that is implemented into mindfulness-based stress reduction (MBSR) courses. I have put my own twist on the exercise as I have seen it do wonders with high-risk adolescents.

Supplies needed: Strawberries or another small fruit that can be passed out to the entire group. When I first implemented this activity in one of my MBA meditation groups, I used small, bite-sized Snickers bars. Yes, I know that is not the healthiest of choices, but the participants were incarcerated and I knew they'd appreciate it. I encourage you use whatever food you deem appropriate; however, I will say that most adolescents seem to get excited about food that tastes good (e.g., candy). Follow these four steps until you have a good sense of the activity and can put your own twist on it:

1. Pass out one bite-sized Snickers bar to each member in the group and alert them to not do anything with it until further instruction.

2. Encourage the group members to close their eyes before beginning to eat their Snickers. If they don't want to close their eyes, it's okay, just encourage them to gaze at the floor in front of them.

3. Next instruct them in the mindful eating activity. Explain to the group that this is a mindfulness activity and that the point is to settle into their experience and slow everything down. Encourage the group to

take at least five small bites of the bite-sized Snickers bar, chewing every bite slowly and fully until the next bite. Repeat about five times until the entire Snickers is gone with eyes closed. Encourage the group members to become aware of any textures, tastes, and anything else they might not ordinarily become aware of when eating fast. Instruct them to breathe and be present to their chewing.

4. When you've noticed everyone in the group to be finished, instruct them to gently open their eyes. Process the experience by encouraging participants to share anything that was different about their eating experience, about any specific details and textures they noticed.

I will never forget the first time I did this activity with a group of incarcerated youth. It was quite successful, as evidenced by one of the participants providing the group with probably the most accurate and detailed description of the contents of a bite-sized Snickers bar. I highly recommend this activity as a method for teaching informal mindfulness and incorporating food into your groups.

Still Chillen

"Still Chillen" is a wonderful game best suited to the group format. It was created by the MBA project and was named by Vinny Ferraro, MBA's training director. The goal of this fun activity is to get youth oriented toward some simple aspects of meditative and mindfulness practice.

Instructions

Have 8–14 adolescents sit either in chairs or on cushions in a circle. Explain to them that they're going to attempt a game in which one cannot move any part of their body, except for breathing and blinking. The object of the game is to be the last person staying completely still. Let the group members know that you will be scanning the group, looking for members who are moving. If anyone moves, you, the facilitator, will call them out and they will have to wait for the next round. Give them about 15–20 seconds after they acknowledge the game rules to get out any laughter, facial expressions, and to stretch. Proceed with a practice round simply to make sure everyone understands the rules and object of the game. Proceed with another round. After that second round, process with the group about the experience. Ask them what "mental muscles" they used in order to not move, what mental techniques or focusing techniques they used to not become distracted.

This activity is a great way to get the blood flowing in the group. It is fun, interactive, and a great learning tool. The main objective is to get the group members thinking about how they may physically sit still after other members have been called out and are potentially distracting. It lends itself to a discussion about how mindfulness may be an avenue to increase self-regulation and responsiveness rather than reactiveness. I have had groups where we've done this activity four or five times. I recommend catering the activity to your specific group. It is a great way to get participants involved and interactive from the start of a group.

Stand If

The final mindfulness-based activity I present in this appendix can be a very deep and heartfelt emotional intelligence and empathy-building exercise. I most often used this exercise under the auspices of my work with MBA; however, this exercise has had many incarnations from multi-cultural and diversity trainings as "cross the line if" activities. Because it has the potential to be a profound experience, the tone for this activity is much more serious than with Still Chillen. The goal of presenting this activity is to foster empathy and courage, to help adolescents understand that others go through similar experiences, and to highlight the idea that the group can be a support for everyone's suffering.

The activity itself involves sitting in a circle and, after the facilitator reads a brief statement, if that statement is true, for group members to stand up for a brief moment. They then sit back down and wait for the facilitator to read another statement. This process is repeated for anywhere from 10–15 statements. The experience is then processed sensitively. Some of the original statements from the MBA curriculum include:

Stand if . . . you have ever been judged because of the style of clothes you wear.
Stand if . . . you have ever felt totally alone.
Stand if . . . you have ever been shot at.

What is imperative is that you cater the sentences to the subcultural population of adolescents you work with. If you work with adolescents at an LGBT clinic, cater the statements to their experience. If you work with adolescents suffering from esteem issues, anger issues, etc., cater the statements for them. I have done this exercise with substance abusing youth and have used some of the following statements:

Stand if . . . you were given drugs as a young child.
Stand if . . . you grew up in a neighborhood in which drugs and alcohol were a problem.
Stand if . . . you use drugs more often than you'd like to.
Stand if . . . you sometimes use drugs to deal with painful feelings.
Stand if . . . you use drugs to forget the past.

A good strategy is to start with more mild, general questions and then progress to deep, personal questions. Having ten questions is good for about a 20-minute experience including processing. Make sure that when you read a statement to let everyone stand, pause, notice who else is standing, and then direct them to sit back down. When you're done, make sure you process the experience with the group. Ask them questions about whether or not they were surprised if anyone stood up, what is was like to share their experiences without saying any words, and of course assess if anyone's past trauma has arisen and needs to be explored.

Because many high-risk adolescents and incarcerated adolescents have similar upbringings, the result of this activity is usually a heightened sense of empathy for other members of the group. I will never forget one of the most powerful experiences I had with this activity while facilitating it in the juvenile detention camp. Two members of the group (of about eight) were rival gang members. I knew it was a huge risk doing this exercise with both of them in the group but decided the advantages outweighed the disadvantages. The two gang members stayed silent throughout the whole experience and did not say anything during the group's processing of the experience. After the group ended, one of the rival gang members stayed back to speak with me confidentially. He disclosed to me that he wanted to have an individual session because he was having thoughts and feelings he had never experienced. He disclosed that for the first time, he felt empathetic toward the rival gang member in the group. He told me that he noticed that he and the other gang member were standing on almost every statement together. It was the beginning of a long contemplation of his place in life and the gang. These two gang members had particularly traumatic upbringings. The Stand If exercise humanized each gang member toward each other, and empathy, even if ever so slightly, resulted. This exercise can also be done standing up in line, or simply sitting classroom-style in chairs and desks. For the most intimate experience, I have found the circle to work best.

Training Resources for
Mental Health Professionals

Below is a list of organizations that offer training and resources regarding incorporating mindfulness into youth work. I have had personal experience with some of these organizations, and others I have simply followed from afar. I apologize for the non-comprehensiveness of the below list, as I am sure there are more wonderful organizations and training centers I do not yet know about.

ENGAGING THE MOMENT, LLC

Web: www.engagingthemoment.com

About: This is my personal business in which I offer continuing education (CE) to mental health professionals. I offer online and in person workshops mostly regarding mindfulness and therapy, working with adolescents, and teaching mindfulness to adolescents.

MIND BODY AWARENESS PROJECT

Web: www.mbaproject.org

About: An Oakland-based non-profit dedicated to bringing mindfulness-based services to at-risk and incarcerated youth. MBA is a premier organization that conducts direct services, research initiatives, and training.

MINDFUL EDUCATION INSTITUTE

Web: www.mindfuleducationinstitute.com

About: Mindful Education Institute (MEI) offers the first year-long training dedicated to teaching therapists, educators, and other mindfulness practitioners how to work effectively with children and adolescents. This training is conducted through retreats and weekly meetings.

MINDFUL SCHOOLS

Web: www.mindfulschools.org

About: Mindful Schools is a non-profit in Oakland, California, that provides mindfulness services in the classroom mostly in elementary schools. Mindful Schools has many online and in-person training opportunities.

IBME (INWARD BOUND EDUCATION)

Web: www.ibme.info

About: iBme offers retreats and trainings for both teens and professionals looking to enhance their skills for working with teens. Retreats are offered in Virginia and California.

STRESSED TEENS

Web: www.stressedteens.com

About: Stressed Teens offers in person and online trainings for mindfulness professionals and for those wishing to learn the Mindfulness-Based Stress Reduction program for teens (MBSR-T).

References

Anayalo. (2010). *Satipatthana: The direct path to realization.* Cambridge, UK: Windhorse Publications.

Baer, R. A. (Ed.). (2006). t*Mindfulness-based treatment approaches: Clinician's guide to evidence base and applications.* San Diego, CA: Elsevier.

Biegel, G. M., Brown, K. W., Shapiro, S. L., & Schubert, C. M. (2009). Mindfulness-based stress reduction for the treatment of adolescent psychiatric outpatients: A randomized clinical trial. *Journal of Consulting and Clinical Psychology, 77*, 855–866.

Bordin, E. S. (1979). The generalizability of the psychoanalytic concept of the working alliance. *Psychotherapy Theory, Research, and Practice, 26*, 17–25.

Bugental, J. F. T. (1965). *The search for authenticity.* New York, NY: Holt, Rinehart, and Winston, Inc.

Bugental, J. F. T. (1987). *The art of the psychotherapist: How to develop the skills that take psychotherapy beyond science.* New York, NY: W. W. Norton & Company, Inc.

Bugental, J. F. T. (1999). *Psychotherapy isn't what you think: Bringing the psychotherapeutic engagement into the living moment.* Phoenix, AZ: Zeig.

Corcoran, J. (1997). A solution-oriented approach to working with juvenile offenders. *Child and Adolescent Social Work Journal, 14*(4), 277–288.

Cotton, S., Larkin, E., Hoopes, A., Cromer, B. A., & Rosenthal, S. L. (2005). The impact of adolescent spirituality on depressive symptoms and health risk behaviors. *Journal of Adolescent Health, 36*, 529.e7–529.e14.

Davis, T. L., Kerr, B. A., & Kerpius, S. E. R. (2003). Meaning, purpose, and religiosity in at-risk youth: The relationship between anxiety and spirituality. *Journal of Psychology and Theology, 31*, 356–365.

Erickson, E. H. (1980). *Identity and the life cycle.* New York, NY: W. W. Norton & Company, Inc.

Evans, W. P., Brown, R., & Killian, E. (2002). Decision making and perceived postdetention success among incarcerated youth. *Crime and Delinquency, 48,* 553–567.

Frankl, V. E. (1959). *Man's search for meaning.* Boston, MA: Beacon Press.

Germer, C. K. (2009). *The mindful path to self-compassion: Freeing yourself from destructive thoughts and emotions.* New York, NY: Guilford Press.

Germer, C. K., Siegel, R., & Fulton, P. R. (Eds.). (2005). *Mindfulness and psychotherapy.* New York, NY: Guilford Press.

Ginsburg, J. I. D., Mann, R. E., Rotgers, F., & Weekes, J. R. (2002). Motivational interviewing with criminal justice populations. In W. R. Miller, & S. Rollnick (Eds.). *Motivational interviewing: Preparing people for change* (pp. 333–347). New York, NY: Guilford Press.

Guerra, N. G., Kim, T. E., & Boxer, P. (2008). What works: Best practices with juvenile offenders. In R. D. Hodge, N. G. Guerra, & P. Boxer (Eds.). *Treating the juvenile offender* (pp. 79–103). New York, NY: Guilford Press.

Henggeler, S. W., Schoenwald, S. K., Borduin, C. M., Rowland, M. D., & Cunningham, P. B. (2009). *Multisystemic therapy for antisocial children and adolescents* (2nd ed.). New York, NY: Guilford Press.

Hick, S. T., & Bien, T. (Eds.). (2008). *Mindfulness and the therapeutic relationship.* New York, NY: Guilford Press.

Himelstein, S. (2011a). Engaging the moment with incarcerated youth: An existential–humanistic approach. *The Humanistic Psychologist, 39,* 206–221.

Himelstein, S. (2011b). Transpersonal psychotherapy with incarcerated adolescents. *Journal of Transpersonal Psychology, 43,* 1–15.

Himelstein, S., & Saul, S. (In preparation). *Mindfulness-based substance abuse treatment for high-risk adolescents: A group-based curriculum.* Manuscript in preparation.

Himelstein, S., Hasting, A. Shapiro, S. L., & Heery, M. (2012a). Mindfulness training for self-regulation and stress with incarcerated youth: A pilot study. *Probation Journal, 59,* 151–165.

Himelstein, S., Hasting, A. Shapiro, S. L., & Heery, M. (2012b). A qualitative investigation of the experience of a mindfulness-based intervention with incarcerated adolescents. *Child and Adolescent Mental Health, 17,* 231–237.

Himelstein, S., Saul, S., Garcia-Romeu, A., & Pinedo, D. (2012c). *Teaching mindfulness to incarcerated adolescents: A pilot grounded theory study.* Manuscript submitted for publication.

Horvath, A., & Symonds, R. D. (1991). Relation between working alliance and outcome in psychotherapy: A meta-analysis. *Journal of Counseling Psychology, 38,* 139–149.

Ingram, B. L. (2006). *Clinical case formulations: Matching the integrative treatment plan to the client.* Hoboken, NJ: John Wiley & Sons, Inc.

Johnston, L. D., O'Malley, P. M., Bachman, J. G., & Schulenberg, J. E. (2012). *Monitoring the Future national survey results on drug use, 1975–2011. Volume*

I: Secondary school students. Ann Arbor, MI: Institute for Social Research, University of Michigan.

Kabat-Zinn, J. (1994). *Wherever you go there you are: Mindfulness meditation in everyday life.* New York, NY: Hyperion.

Kornfield, J. (2008). *The wise heart: A guide to the universal teachings of Buddhist psychology.* New York, NY: Bantam Books.

Martin, D. J., Graske, J. P., & Davis, M. K. (2000). Relation of the therapeutic alliance with outcome and other variables: A meta-analytic review. *Journal of Consulting and Clinical Psychology, 68,* 438–450.

May, R. (1969). *Love and will.* New York, NY: Delta.

McLeod, B. D. (2011). Relation of the alliance with outcomes in youth psychotherapy: A meta-analysis. *Clinical Psychology Review, 31,* 603–616.

Miller, W. R., & Rollnick, S. (2002). *Motivational interviewing: Preparing people for change* (2nd ed.). New York, NY: Guilford Press.

Prochaska, J. O., & DiClemente, C. C. (1984). *The transtheoretical approach: Crossing the traditional boundaries of therapy.* Malabar, FL: Krieger.

Safran, J. D., & Muran, J. C. (2000) *Negotiating the therapeutic alliance: A relational treatment guide.* New York, NY: Guilford Press.

Schaeffer, C. M., & Borduin, C. M. (2005). Long-term follow-up to a randomized clinical trial of multisystemic therapy with serious and violent juvenile offenders. *Journal of Consulting and Clinical Psychology, 73,* 445–453.

Shapiro, S. L., & Carlson, L. E. (2009). *The art and science of mindfulness: Integrating mindfulness into psychology and the helping professions.* Washington, DC: American Psychological Association.

Shirk, S. R., & Karver, M. (2003). Prediction of treatment outcome from relationship variables in child and adolescent therapy: A meta-analytic review. *Journal of Consulting and Clinical Psychology, 71,* 452–464.

Sibinga, E. M., Stewart, M., Magyarhi, T., Welsh, C. K., Hutton, N., & Ellen, J. M. (2007). Mindfulness-based stress reduction for HIV-infected youth: A pilot study. *Explore, 4,* 36–37.

Siegel, D. J. (2010). *The mindful therapist: A clinician's guide to mindsight and neural integration.* New York, NY: W. W. Norton & Company, Inc.

Steiner, H., Garcia, I. G., & Matthews, Z. (1997). Posttraumatic stress disorder in incarcerated juvenile delinquents. *Journal of the Academy of Child and Adolescent Psychiatry, 36,* 357–365.

Surrey, J. L. (2005). Relational psychotherapy, relational mindfulness. In C. K. Germer, R. D. Siegel, & P. R. Fulton (Eds.). *Mindfulness and psychotherapy* (pp. 91–113). New York, NY: Guilford Press.

Suzuki, S. (1998). *Zen mind beginner's mind: Informal talks on Zen meditation and practice.* New York, NY: Weatherhill.

Taffel, R. (2005). *Breaking through to teens: Psychotherapy for the new adolescence.* New Nork, NY: Guilford Press.

Veysey, B. M. (2008). Mental health, substance abuse, and trauma. In R. D. Hodge, N. G. Guerra, & P. Boxer (Eds.). *Treating the juvenile offender* (pp. 210–239). New York, NY: Guilford Press.

Vitacco, M. J., Neumann, C. S., Robertson, A. A., & Durrant, S. L. (2002). Contributions of impulsivity and callousness in the assessment of adjudicated male adolescents: A prospective study. *Journal of Personality Assessment, 78,* 87–103.

Wall, R. B. (2005). Tai chi and mindfulness-based stress reduction in a Boston middle school. *Journal of Pediatric Health Care, 19,* 230–237.

Wong, Y. J., Rew, L., & Slaikeu, K. D. (2006). A systematic review of recent research on adolescent religiosity/spirituality and mental health. *Issues in Mental Health Nursing, 27,* 161–183.

Yalom, I. D. (1980). *Existential psychotherapy.* New York, NY: Basic Books.

Yalom, I. D. (2002). *The gift of therapy: An open letter to a new generation of therapist and their patients.* New York, NY: HarperCollins Publishers, Inc.

Yalom, I. D. (2005). *Theory and practice of group psychotherapy* (5th ed.). New York, NY: Basic Books.

Index

acceptance 13, 41, 62, 86–87, 131, 146–147
accountability 28, 47
acculturation 112
acting out 23, 92
activities 171–177
actual 129–141, 150
advocacy 111, 128
agenda setting 126
aggression 44, 50–52, 59, 125
aikido 50–53
alcohol 91, 97, 176
Alcoholics Anonymous 62
Alex 81–84, 93
Alice 149–150, 156–157
Allport-Ross Religious Orientation Scale 79
American Psychological Association (APA) 22
analytic therapy 28
Anayalo 131–132
Anicca 17, 94
anxiety 6, 11, 33, 45, 47–50; core themes 93; eliciting awareness 133, 136; group facilitation 109; resistance 57–58, 60; spirituality 77, 79–80
applications 4–19
archetypes 30, 87

assessment 9, 15, 35, 38, 138
assumptions 61
authenticity 7–8, 12, 25–26, 28–30, 32–38; core themes 91, 96, 98, 102–103; eliciting awareness 131–134, 136, 138–139, 141; goals 150; group facilitation 107–108, 110, 113; meditation 156, 158; paradox of change 61–62, 65–68, 70–71, 73–74; relationships 21–41; resistance 44–49, 53, 57, 59–60; role 150, 159; spirituality 78, 84–88; teaching 143–144, 147
autonomy 9, 11–12, 56–57, 90–92, 99–103; eliciting awareness 130–131; paradox of change 67–68; spirituality 80

backlashes 119
backward regression method 79
barriers 34, 62, 65, 108
beginner's-mind sphere 28–29, 37, 125–126, 149
behavioral change 9, 61, 65–73, 88, 108, 121, 130
best interests of clients 35–37, 41, 50, 156
bias 60, 110, 146–147, 159

curiosity 9, 28–29, 33, 37, 55;
eliciting awareness 130; goals
148; group facilitation 125
curriculum 46, 107, 109, 123, 125;
exercises 168, 175; role 154

data gathering 77, 90, 125, 127, 134
Davis, T.L. 79
death 13–14, 16–17, 62, 78, 81–84;
anxiety 93–94, 96; core themes
90, 101–103; eliciting awareness
139; spirituality 88; teaching role
147
deep-breathing meditation 162–163
deep-listening sphere 29–32
defense mechanisms 45–46, 87–88,
93
deflection 33
denial 67, 84, 93
dharma 6, 94; dharmas 132–133, 136
DiClemente, C.C. 66–67
disclaimers 65–73
diversity of experience 116, 125–126

eating exercises 173–174
economics 13, 81, 128
Eddie 29–30
ego 44–45, 57, 60, 88, 93; eliciting
awareness 132; group facilitation
124; teaching role 147
eliciting awareness 150
emotions 6, 16–18, 46–47, 49, 58;
core themes 91, 94–95, 99,
101–102; eliciting awareness
129–130, 132–136, 140; goals
151; group facilitation 109,
115–116, 123; meditation 155;
teaching 145, 147
empathy 34, 37, 99, 150, 176–177
Engaging the Moment 179
Erikson, E. 78
ethics 67
evidence-based therapy 3, 22–23
exercises 145–146, 149, 161–177

existentialism 4, 10, 35, 68, 79–80,
82, 94
expectations 25–27, 38, 109, 117
experiments 21, 51, 152
externalization 23–24, 73

facial expression 26, 133, 174
facilitation of groups 107–128, 153,
159
faith 109–110
feedback 85, 113–114, 127–128,
147, 155
feeling tone 132, 137–138, 141
feelings 31, 33, 35–37, 40, 45; core
themes 97–100, 102; eliciting
awareness 130, 134–137,
140–141; exercises 176; goals
150; group facilitation 115, 121,
127; paradox of change 70–73;
resistance 47–50, 53, 55, 57–59;
spirituality 82–87
females 79, 91
Ferraro, V. 109–110, 174
flow 33, 128
focus groups 64–65, 127–128
football 69–70, 72, 95–96
formal techniques 3–4, 151–152,
157–158, 161–162
foundations 6, 9–10, 12, 19–20, 53;
core themes 89; eliciting
awareness 131–141; paradox of
change 67, 74
Frager, R. 50–51
France 29
Frank 139–141
future directions 21

gangs 8, 10–13, 15–17, 38, 93;
eliciting awareness 140; exercises
176–177; group facilitation 120;
meditation 152
Garcia, I.G. 13
gatekeepers 111
Germer, C.K. 3, 7

trust 26–27, 29–33, 36, 38, 41;
  group facilitation 107, 111–112,
  117, 120; meditation 152;
  paradox of change 71; resistance
  49, 56

Ueishiba, M. 50
unconscious 41, 44–45, 91
United States (US) 29, 139
University of Denver 23
University of Michigan 90

Vickie 54–55
victimization 46
violence 13–14, 93–94, 114, 118, 120
vulnerability 34, 46, 87–88

Wayne 55–56, 63–64
weight-training metaphor 154
West 45, 50, 132, 173
withholding information 121
witnessing 29–32, 88, 132
Wong, Y.J. 80
workshops 79
worldview 14, 17, 44, 53, 77–89;
  core themes 103; eliciting
  awareness 138; teaching role 143,
  159

Yalom, I.D. 35, 37, 93, 111
Youth Risk Behavior Survey 80

zen 29